Robert D. McClinchey
with Gregory W. McClinchey

Jack of All Trades and Master of None

an inventory of my life and times

iUniverse, Inc.
Bloomington

iUniverse books may be ordered through booksellers or by contacting:

iUniverse
1663 Liberty Drive
Bloomington, IN 47403
www.iuniverse.com
1-800-Authors (1-800-288-4677)

ISBN: 978-1-4759-4024-4 (sc)
ISBN: 978-1-4759-4026-8 (hc)
ISBN: 978-1-4759-4025-1 (e)

Printed in the United States of America

iUniverse rev. date: 8/9/2012

TO MISS FRANCES

CONTENTS

Author's Note

When first approached with the idea of writing my memoirs, I was a little apprehensive as to whether I had the literary skills required to put together an interesting and readable collection. Despite my initial misgivings and armed with the encouragement of my friends and family, I decided to give it a try.

The following pages contain the fruits of my labours, something I have intended for the enjoyment of my family, relatives, friends and acquaintances. These pages contain my recollections as they relate to specific, real-life events, reminiscences and conversations that span the time period between my birth in 1926 and the present day. In essence, these pages contain a collection of stories that outline selected facets of my life, my numerous occupations and the countless people whom I have had the privilege to know and interact with.

Without my now-departed wife and soul mate, and without the ongoing support of my family, I would never have had my memories, both good and bad, generated as a result of our time together. And without those memories, this book would never have been possible.

With this in mind, I am indebted to several people for their friendship, advice and assistance, and in particular I would like to mention my son, Wayne, for his willingness to share his musical talent over the years. I would also like to thank my grandson, Greg, for his expert advice and for his many hours spent writing and formulating these memoirs.

I truly hope and trust that my efforts will meet with your approval and that the pages to follow will cause fond remembrances and perhaps even a smile or two. If this is the case, then my efforts will have been richly rewarded.

Thanks for the memories,

Robert D. McClinchey

FOREWORD

Greg McClinchey, grandson

I first met Robert McClinchey in April 1976, and while I have no recollection of that initial encounter, it touched off a lasting personal association that has spanned nearly 37 years.

In 2012 Robert McClinchey turned 86, and in doing so he began yet another chapter in a life that has, thus far, been colourful, diverse and worthy of note, to say the least. Whether he was a farmer; a bus driver; a mechanic; a musician; or a restaurateur, Robert McClinchey has lived his life in a style that has clearly earned him the respect and esteem of all those he encountered.

Although he is not a man of traditional wealth, political influence or excessive formal education, Robert McClinchey has, as a student of life, proven an aptitude for real-world adaptability, problem solving and people management. He is, in every sense of the word, a true polymath.

His impact has been felt by many over the years, but to me, Bob McClinchey is an example, a mentor and a teacher of things. He taught me how to play the spoons; how to make a whistle out of a willow branch; and how a person can deal with difficulty and adversity while maintaining a definitive sense of humour and inner calm. He has shown me that age is nothing more than a number, something to be worn as a decoration rather than as an albatross. He exemplifies experience and know-how; he exudes acceptance and hospitality; and he is the epitome of what every grandfather should be.

I say this because, for as long as I can remember, Robert McClinchey has embodied everything I have aspired to become. He was and is a hardworking, goodhearted and productive member of his community; a respected and trusted confidant; and a loving and devoted son, husband, father, grandfather and great-grandfather.

While I may not have known him in his earliest of days, I am confident that I know Robert McClinchey in his most refined and complete incarnation. Despite this, there are still large gaps in my knowledge of the life and times of this man—a man who happens to be a fifth-generation Canadian and the patriarch of the McClinchey family. For those with whom his path has crossed over the past 86 years, the pages of this book will help shed a new light on this complex person. Details of his childhood, his personal relationships, his employment history, his aspirations and even his regrets are, for the first time ever, chronicled in the pages to follow. And although he is not someone who has radically altered the course of history, his grasp of the human condition makes this account well worth the read.

Whether you know him as Robert, Bob, Pa, Grandpa or even as Cactus Mack, there is no mistaking his infectious laugh, his calm demeanour or his indelible expression as he deliberately draws a bow across his well-tuned Stainer or Louis Lowendall. After a life that has been, in many ways, stylistically analogous to the fictional accountings of Tom Sawyer, Robert McClinchey is now adding the title of author to his accomplished pedigree.

I am truly honoured to have been part of the chapters spanning the past 37 years and am as eager to learn about the details contained in those prior to that as I am to help write the chapters yet to come.

A FALL OFF THE MANGEL WAGON

When you look back at your life, the greatest
happinesses are family happinesses.
—Dr. Joyce Brothers

I was born quite young on a frosty Tuesday, January 19, 1926. As was the custom at the time, I was born at home on the farm rather than in a hospital, as commonly happens today. My father, Edward Gordon McClinchey (1899–1989), was the second-youngest son of John McClinchey and his wife, Julia Daer, of Irish/German descent. On the other side of the family tree, my mother, Lillian Dell Anderson (1904–1988), was the daughter of William Anderson and Florence Patterson, who were of English and Scottish ancestry, respectively. Together, through the Great Depression and WWII, my father and mother raised a happy and healthy family of five boys and two girls. In addition to me, the McClinchey family eventually consisted of Eileen Florence (July 22, 1927), William John (May 25, 1929), Lillian Jewel (March 25, 1933), Norman Gordon (July 14, 1935), David Edward (April 25, 1940) and John Currie (November 7, 1944).

In my much younger days at home.

Mother and Father celebrate their fiftieth wedding anniversary at the Auburn Hall in November 1975. Their children stand with them (Left to right: Norman, Eileen, Robert, Lillian (Mother), John, Gordon (Father), David, Jewel and Bill).

My earliest memories of home take me back to our simple life of a hundred-acre farm two miles north of Auburn, on Lot 28, Concession 3 of East Wawanosh Township (83609 Donnybrook Line, Auburn). Today that same farm is owned by my brother Norman McClinchey and his wife, Lila. But before Norman assumed ownership of the family homestead, it was my mother who used her formidable skills and talents as a former schoolteacher to corral and wrangle her energetic children, to care for a busy husband and to keep a house for a growing and rambunctious family. She was a tremendous homemaker, and looking back I have often wondered how she managed to do it all so effectively without using the many modern household conveniences and gadgets, such as a freezer, an automatic washer, a refrigerator or a microwave, many of which are taken for granted by today's families.

As the wife of a busy farmer, in addition to her role as mother, nurse and primary caregiver to seven children, my mother never failed to prepare three hearty meals each and every day. This, coupled with the ongoing necessity of churning butter; canning and preserving fruits, vegetables and meats for the winter months; and washing and repairing a never-ending pile of clothes meant the days were long and arduous. Despite this endless to-do list, my parents always made time for family.

Circa 1950: Father works with the team of horses to finish the daily chores on the home farm north of Auburn while Norman and John look on.

For example, once the work was done on Saturday nights, we would all head to Auburn where my brothers, sisters and I would receive our weekly allowance of 10 or 15 cents. With our pockets jingling full of our newfound wealth, we would dash off to the store where a five-cent ice cream cone, or perhaps some liquorice candy, awaited us. This was also the day when Mom and Dad would socialize with the neighbours and stock up on essential household supplies for the week ahead.

But Saturday night was not the only time when the McClinchey family headed to town. After the chores were done early each Sunday morning, the entire family would don our Sunday best, harness the team and head off to Sunday school and Sunday service at the nearby Auburn United Church. Following the homily, we would spend the rest of the day visiting friends and relatives, enjoying fiddle music and filling up on home cooking and fellowship for all. Put another way, we were building memories that were to last a lifetime.

Circa 1931: Bill, Bob and Eileen McClinchey as toddlers.

One of my earliest childhood memories stems from when I was very young, perhaps 2 or 3 years old. My mother and father were taking up mangels near the back end of the farm and loading them onto a wagon. There was a time when mangels were a common crop, but for those who may not be old enough to know what mangels are, they are also known as "fodder beets." Mangels are very easy to grow, producing large roots that store well. The mangel roots grow quite large, in some cases up to two feet long, and in days gone by, these hearty roots were used as a staple food for cattle. In emergency situations, the roots and leaves could be prepared for human consumption in a way not unlike the sugar beet. Father always grew a few rows of mangels to pulp for cattle feed, and every night each of the horses received a mangel to munch on as a reward for the day's work. He even split a couple for the hens to pick at as he claimed they were good for their digestive systems.

On one of our many mangel-pulling days, I guess Father and Mother forgot about me playing on and around the wagon, and as they advanced the wagon down the row, a small thump and a loud whimper quickly jogged their memories. On that particular occasion I had opted to play in the path of the wagon, and to my detriment, I quickly found myself under a heavily loaded mangel wagon. All jokes aside about falling off the turnip—or mangel—truck, my mother was less than impressed with the entire ordeal. I still remember her frantically gathering me up and carrying me the entire way back to the house, followed by an eventual checkup with Dr. Weir. Although my injuries were not critical or apparently long-lasting, I vividly remember a sharp pain on the left side of my body. Today, despite the subsequent eighty-plus years since my run-in with a mangel wagon, I still have a clear memory and an occasional weakness on my left side as a result of that day. Given what might have been, I guess I should consider myself pretty lucky that I am still here to pen this story.

In 1975, the entire family (spouses included) came together for Mother and Father's fiftieth anniversary. (Back from the left: John & Maureen McClinchey; Norman & Lila McClinchey; George & Eileen Haggitt; Bob & Fran McClinchey; Dave & Ruth McClinchey; Alvin & Jewel Plunkett; and Bill & Bev McClinchey).

A TRIP TO THE CELLAR

He didn't tell me how to live; he lived, and let me watch him do it.
—Clarence Budington Kelland

My father was tough but fair, and generally it wasn't a good idea to cross him. He was certainly not unjust or mean, but my brothers, sisters and I knew the rules, and more to the point, we know what would almost certainly happen once Father learned of any transgressions should we decide to step over the line. With the benefit of hindsight, I have to respect him for his even and reasoned temperament, even if I didn't really appreciate these virtues at the time. In the same vein, I drew many of my other life lessons from my father, whether I knew it at the time or not. Just as I would eventually become, my father was really a jack of all trades, something you had to be in those days if you were to be a successful farmer. Unlike modern farming operations, a breakdown in the 1920s, '30s or '40s was something that was usually dealt with on-site, by the farmer, rather than by an outside expert or specialist. With time, money and the availability of certain outside skills all in limited supply, survival required Father to be a mechanic, a machinist, a mill operator, a labourer and a herdsman all rolled into one.

In addition to his own chores and responsibilities, my father never failed to help our neighbours butcher cattle, doctor sick animals or deal with other on-farm emergencies as they developed.

I remember one such instance when Billie Boyle, who operated the General Store in St. Augustine, found himself stuck in a sinkhole on the side road not far from our gate. Being early spring, the frost was almost gone and the gravel roads were pretty soft in places. As a result, father had a near full-time job pulling cars out of the mud with his team of horses. In the case of Billie Boyle, he joked that the McClinchey family must make a pretty penny by pulling passersby out of this wet and muddy hole night and day.

My father, never one to miss an opportunity for a quip, replied, "We don't pull anyone out at night because that is when we haul the water to muddy the road …"

Billie scoffed as if to sarcastically suggest that he believed what Father was saying. Father howled with laughter and went back to his work. My father had a very active sense of humour and never took himself or his work too seriously. Perhaps that is why he lived such a long and healthy life.

Norman McClinchey and Father (Gordon McClinchey) cut hay on the home farm.

Another of my father's distractions, perhaps an even greater one than his unique sense of humour, was his love of music and, in particular, fiddle music. He was known to occasionally grab the fiddle and play for a house party or a dance if asked. He was quite a capable amateur player for certain, but with a glass or two of the right liquid lubrication under his belt (unbeknownst to Mother), his playing was elevated to a whole new level. In later years, as a fiddle player myself, I have come to appreciate the value of a small nip while playing for or with friends. In Father's case, the choice drink of the day was a well-aged apple cider. Father always had a 40-gallon barrel on hand for emergencies. When a neighbour or two arrived at the door for an impromptu card game, the first thing that appeared was a pitcher of the good stuff. He also kept a batch of dandelion wine on the go as a back-up ... just in case.

As a kid, I have more than a couple of memories of our secret trips to the cellar for a sample sip from the bottles stashed carefully on the shelves. One day, I even recall Father telling his hired man that his dandelion wine must be evaporating through the corks so he'd put a pencil mark on the bottle to monitor that "evaporation" a bit more closely. In hindsight, I am absolutely sure he knew very well what was causing the unexplained evaporation, but he opted to give us a little leeway. In any event, we were much more careful, and a little more creative, during our less frequent trips to the cellar. Armed with our newfound understanding of Father's monitoring system, and a pencil of our own, we simply adjusted the pencil marks on each bottle following each visit. Despite our ingenuity, I suspect he knew what was actually afoot although he never admitted it, nor did he question us about it.

Father was also particular in his organizational approach. He was quite strict about putting a fork, shovel, hammer or any other tool back in its proper place once they were no longer required for the job at hand. He expected a dirty shovel to be cleaned thoroughly before it was returned to the shed or barn, and he could be quite crusty if he later found an improperly cleaned tool hanging in its place. As a child, I was more than once found guilty of this terrible crime, but with the benefit of a few more years' experience, I now appreciate and have adopted his meticulous approach to tool care in my own life. I may even have passed it along to my own son. I guess the apple never falls too far from the cider jug.

Poor Pete

If variety is the spice of life, then recreation is the sugar.
—Kimberly Grandal

In the days before radio and television, one of the McClinchey family's favourite winter recreational activities involved each other and music. Once our chores and supper were done, the entire family would retire to the parlour to play some old-time, toe-tapping, family-gathering music before bed. Father would take the lead on the fiddle, Mother would tickle the ivories of the piano and I would strum away on a guitar—or whatever else was available at the time. This evening "music time" at home served as the backdrop to some of my favourite memories growing up and, in many ways, that important tradition has lived on into my own family and home life years later. Just as I passed many enjoyable evenings with my father and mother in this way, as a parent myself I was often known to take to the fiddle, my wife to the piano and my son to the guitar for an evening of memories and enjoyment. That love of old-time music, instilled in me as a child, is, for me, a defining aspect of my life in my youth and throughout my adult years.

In addition to music, given that work was such an important part of life on the farm, we also tried to find fun wherever we were. To help with the work, my father hired a man to help with the labour until his children were old enough to be useful on the farm. The hired man's name was Norman Wilson and Norm stayed with us for seven years. In this time period, Auburn had a championship baseball team and Norm was their catcher. Between chores, in the evenings and on certain select Sundays, I used to catch the ball for him when he practised. I am not sure how good I actually was, but I suspect that playing with Norm taught me to love baseball, a sport that remains a favourite of mine to this day.

Norm Wilson ready for a game.

In addition to his abilities on the diamond, Norm was also good with horses. In those days, the plowing, cultivating and most other heavy farm work was done with a team of large Clydesdale horses. These horses weighed upward of a ton each, and with the distinctive personalities of each animal at play, it took a skilled and patient hand to make them do what was expected of them. In addition to the Clydesdales, Father also kept a team of light horses for sleigh and cutter work and to deliver the mail. As a way of augmenting the family income, Father regularly delivered the mail on Rural Route #2, out of Auburn. Beginning in Auburn and heading north to St. Augustine, west through Dungannon and then back to Auburn, the 30-mile trip was often marred by snow, blizzards, hail, heavy rain and sweltering heat, but as the saying goes, the mail must get through. I remember several days when Father would be as late as 11:00 p.m. arriving home from the mail route for supper. These were the difficult realities of rural living in those days.

Similarly, I remember when one of our heavy horses, the one we called Pete, developed lockjaw and couldn't eat or drink.

Circa 1940: Bill McClinchey sits atop Pete.

In the 1940s there was no cure for lockjaw, so after a couple of weeks, Pete passed away. Unfortunately, the concept of an external dead-stock removal service was still several years away, so when an animal died, large or small, it had to be disposed of on-farm—by hand. I can still remember Father and Norm digging a grave, with hand shovels, for hours in an effort to excavate a hole big enough to accommodate Pete's tremendously large frame. After nearly an entire day's work, the imposing hill on the north side of the barn became Pete's final resting place. The loss of an animal like that was a horrible blow to the entire farming operation, especially given the difficult times associated with the Great Depression. Despite this, we needed to continue, and as he always did Father fixed the problem in a matter of days by acquiring Pete's successor. Depression or no depression, there was no time to waste.

Fiddling to the Mill

I never did a day's work in my life. It was all fun.
—Thomas A. Edison

The Maitland River ran by our home farm and served as a nearby source of fun and recreation. From the front door of the house it was just a five-minute walk for swimming, picnicking or fishing, the latter of which being one of my favourite pastimes as a child and as an adult.

The McClinchey family enjoys the Maitland River.

The river was a great place to wash up and cool off after a long day spent harvesting or haying in the summer sun. There was a big rock in the centre of the river that was perfectly set as a diving platform and place to cast a line from. Black bass were plentiful and were a frequent catch, much to Father's delight. He claimed that black bass were the best pan fish going. In addition to bass, we used to catch the odd rainbow trout where the stream entered the river and we could quite often catch enough speckled trout for a meal from the streams within walking distance of the farm. The Maitland River was one of the best local places to fish, and unlike today its clean water was a great source of countless hours of fishing and splashing for my brothers and me.

Those same hot and humid days that we loved as children also presented a challenge for our parents. In the days before household refrigeration and electric lighting, most of the neighbours belonged to a "beef ring." In simple terms, a beef ring is a group of neighbours who formed an association whereas they could have fresh beef delivered to their homes throughout the summer months. Each week one of the farmers in the group would supply a suitable animal to be slaughtered and divided among the members of the ring. Each family would have meat bags with their name on them, and the person who supplied the animal would be responsible for delivering the meat to the rest of the group. As an additional "perk" the person supplying the animal would also be permitted to keep the heart, liver and various other desirable yet limited parts. Today this might not be seen as a bonus, but in those days, the iron- and protein-rich organ meat was a real treat that was in relative short supply. To my recollection, the communal slaughterhouse was just west of St. Augustine and the butcher of choice was Tom Webster. His job was to slaughter and prepare the animal and then divide the spoils appropriately and fairly between all members of the beef ring. I can still remember going with my father to ensure that these bags of meat were delivered to all the neighbours when our turn came. In many ways, I wonder if it was the diversity of these early years that led me toward a jack-of-all-trades approach to life in my later years.

As the summer months faded and winter began to emerge, as kids we always looked forward to wagon or sleigh rides to the nearby community of Auburn. Often the trip was to the grist mill to have our grain ground so it could be used for cattle feed. The mill's giant grinding wheel, which was owned and operated by Harold Bogie until 1944, was powered entirely by water in those early years. Subsequent to that, between 1944 and 1953, the mill was under the ownership and day-to-day management of Warner Andrews. In an effort to achieve greater efficiency and reliability, Warner installed a diesel engine, which was used to power the mill until its eventual demise under the ownership of Worthy McNee.

I remember it costing about five cents to grind a bag of grain and it was not unusual for the entire process to take several hours. Often, while we were waiting for the chop to be ready, we would call on George Hamilton, a friend of Father's who lived nearby. Mr. Hamilton played the fiddle and usually had a generous supply of well-aged cider on hand. Of course these factors attracted my father, a man who enjoyed both the fiddle and cider. Mr. Hamilton and my father would joke back and forth about the barrel number of the cider, and after several songs and multiple pitchers of the good stuff, we would head out to pick up the chop and then go home. Father always seemed to be in much better twist during the trip home.

In addition to transporting grain to the Auburn mill, each autumn we ferried wagonloads of apples to the local apple evaporator. The apples were dried and then packaged for shipment to Europe. We traditionally had a large orchard on the farm, but in the spring of 1934, after a warm spell, the outside temperature plummeted to well-below freezing. The shock killed 80 percent of the local apple trees, which prompted a dramatic reduction in local apple yields. Lack of product prompted the evaporator to permanently close in 1934, forever halting our related outings to Auburn.

After that, we only visited Mr. Hamilton during stopovers at the grist mill.

A Pox on the House

If I'd known I was going to live so long, I'd
have taken better care of myself.
—Leon Eldred

Autumn on the farm was always a busy time. In particular, work bees to process and preserve seasonal food and condiments such as horseradish, the pickling of sauerkraut and general butchering always brought friends and neighbours together in a neighbour-helping-neighbour approach to socializing. Large gardens were the norm in those days, so canning and pickling efforts were in full swing by the fall. Similarly, in the spring when the fish were spawning, we were always on hand to net suckers, mullet and shad (river herring). Then, after our nets were filled to the limit, we would take the fish home by the tub, where they would remain until they were cleaned, washed, sliced and put into sealers with a vinegar solution and canned. These fish were notorious for their small bones, but the vinegar would dissolve and soften them. Then, as a result of this work during the spring, summer and fall, during the harsher winter months we would enjoy a bounty each night for our evening meal. It was a different time—one that did not offer processed food, microwave dinners or easily imported fruits and vegetable from far-off tropical places. Food was hearty, and for the most part the living was relatively simple and generally healthy.

I do remember when that healthy living once took a decided turn for the worse. One winter in particular, nearly every child in our house developed varicella zoster virus approximately three weeks apart. This terrible virus, also known as chickenpox, seemed disastrous at the time,

19

but looking back it may have been one of the best things that ever happened to me. I must have been seven or eight when I was struck down with hundreds of itchy spots. To a kid, chickenpox is a horror but my mother, the former teacher, took it as an opportunity for me to learn something new. Given that I was quarantined in the house as the virus ran its course, Mother started to show me the basic chords on the piano. With three weeks of idle time and a mother who refused to give up, it wasn't long before I was chording to Father's fiddle tunes. Then, as my proficiency increased, I graduated to old-time dance music and eventually was roped into playing at dances, social functions and family gatherings. In many cases I was substituted in for my mother, so I often wondered if there was an ulterior motive to the apparent madness she demonstrated when she opted to teach me how to play the piano. In any event, this opened a musical door to me that would be a major factor for the rest of my life. From the lessons my mother gave me during my bout with chickenpox through to several piano lessons I took at the hands of a stern music teacher named Professor Alf Cook—lessons that cost only 50 cents each (hardly enough to pay for the teacher's shoe leather he wore out walking to his various appointment)—music was to be my lifelong partner. But despite my success with piano lessons, I had always longed to play the fiddle, just as my father and his father before him played.

My father's fiddle was his pride and joy, and as a result, we were never permitted to touch it—ever. This hands-off policy presented obvious challenges for anyone wanting to learn how to play the instrument. Knowing of my unwavering desire to play, on my 30th birthday, Father gave me an old fiddle to practise on and to learn with. I was elated and subsequently launched my efforts to learn the instrument. At about the same time, my mother's brother, Uncle Tom Anderson, gave me his fiddle—a nice Stainer—as a Christmas gift. While I enjoyed and played both of these instruments for many years, I later gave Uncle Tom Anderson's fiddle to his grandchildren, who were also quite musical. They continue to play it and enjoy it to this very day.

As much as my journey toward the fiddle sounds a bit disjointed and strange, it can't hold a candle to the unusual lengths to which my father had to go to learn the craft during his youth. My paternal grandmother was an odd woman in that she did not permit music of any kind in the house. Because of this prohibition, and due to the fact that my father slept upstairs when he was a boy, in the event he wanted to practise the fiddle he needed to tie a rope to it and then gently lower it from his window to the ground outside. Then, after he slipped out of the house himself, he would retrieve his forbidden instrument and rendezvous at the neighbour's house for a secret practice session. Grandma McClinchey always said that all music, in particular fiddle music, was the work of the Devil and had no place in any truly Christian home. Of course this was the same woman who vehemently rebuffed any suggestion she might temporarily care for her grandchildren by sternly declaring, "You brought them into this world so you can take care of them." As a result of this abnormal detachment from her family, I rarely saw her and knew little about her life. I guess that is the unfortunate reality in some families.

WILF, HARVEY AND ME

If you obey all the rules you miss all the fun.
—Katharine Hepburn

Father enjoyed a good time, and as a result he was blessed with many good friends. One of those friends lived near Auburn and went by the name of Harvey McGee. Like my father, Harvey enjoyed a good time filled with music, friends and an occasional glass of aged cider. Harvey was well-known for his ability to sing Scottish and Irish songs, and when performing at concerts, Harvey usually dressed in a kilt and tam (also known as a Balmoral or a Glengarry hat). Harvey had an outlandish personality that helped him be a memorable performer, a skilled musician and a fantastically funny master of ceremonies or host.

Harvey McGee with his wife (Helen) and their dog.

Periodically during the cold winter nights, there would be amateur concerts at the old Forester's Hall in Auburn. Basically the organizers would round up the local talent and put on a music and variety show by and for the locals. I was lucky enough to be asked to join in the fun at one of these concerts, and in keeping with the custom, lighthearted and often funny banter or teasing ensued between the performers and the audience. During the evening of my illustrious debut, Harvey decided to poke a little fun at my father, who was widely known for his sense of humour. Harvey asked me, "Why is your voice changing?" to which I uttered the preplanned response, "Because I cracked my voice crying for bread when I was young." Despite his generally accepted sense of humour, Father seemed to miss the timely gag and hostilely replied,

"There is no damn way you ever had to cry for bread." I guess these things always seem a little funnier when they are directed at someone else.

That concert was a memorable time for me, and not just because of the joke. In fact, I truly enjoyed the camaraderie and showmanship of the stage. As I think back, I can still remember the song I sang, an old Wilf Carter tune, "There's a Love Knot in My Lariat."

I'll be thinking of you, pal, at sunset time
Thinking of the happy days gone by
There beneath those dear old western skies
And I'll tell you just the reason why,

Harvey sang some great songs, such as "Wee Deoch an' Doris" and "She's the Lass for Me." I can even remember a few lines from this last one. It went:

She's the lass for me; she's the lass for me.
I've never seen another face that could ever take her place.
She has locked my heart and stole away the key.
She is, yes she is, she is the lass for me.

When Harvey sang these songs, it didn't get much better than that.

A SMELLY LESSON LEARNED

*Be at war with your vices, at peace with your neighbours
and let every New Year find you a better man.*
—Benjamin Franklin

In the 1930s, '40s and '50s, the only available social support systems
came in the form of a strong community. Your neighbours were more
than just the people who lived next to you. They were also the people
who helped you when you were down; they helped when you needed
them and you reciprocated whenever you could. Put another way, even
if your neighbours were not always your cup of tea, good manners
and necessity dictated that a friendship would take hold regardless
of any minor warts or blemishes. For the most part, folks were good
and kind and genuinely wanted to live by the creed "do unto others as
you would have them do unto you." But despite this required affinity,
this arrangement also provided numerous out-of-the-ordinary and
downright weird couplings that offered substantial flavour up and
down the concessions roads.

One such example would have to be Ernie and Mable
Hickingbottom. Ernie and Mable were an unmarried brother and sister
duo who, for whatever reason, decided to spend their lives together, as a
single bachelor and unwed spinster. While they were truly kind, Ernie
was an exceptionally capable moocher.

Ernie always carried a pipe with a big bowl, and if he ever saw
someone with extra tobacco in hand he would inevitably outstretch his
hand and beg, "You couldn't spare a little tobacco?" Once you handed
over your pouch, he would tap his pipe as full as possible and then dig

half of it back out. He would put the "excess" into his pocket for later use, and then, as if to taunt, he would say, "I have a brand new package in my pocket but I just hate like hell to open it." He used the same tactic with chewing tobacco, especially at a threshing bee (a threshing bee is a term used to describe when neighbours gather together for a collective work effort such as threshing grain).

Mable didn't hit the chewing tobacco, but she was one of the most prolific chain smokers I have ever known. I recall that the end of her nose was permanently discoloured, stained with the nicotine of a thousand cigarettes. For the most part no one noticed, but one day at a threshing bee Jack Armstrong changed all that. Jack was planning to stay for dinner, and just as Mable opened the door to the oven, about two inches of her charred cigarette fell from her mouth into the freshly cooked pan of roast beef. Jack recoiled and blurted out, "By the Jesus, that sure didn't do much to whet my appetite." Quiet snickers filled the room, but Mable just ignored the commotion and moved on—feeding a house full of hungry men. In those days, you often just ignored things like that.

Continuing with the Ernie and Mable saga, one summer day as I was sitting at home my mother received a distressed telephone call from Mable. As neighbours, it was not uncommon that a call for help would come in and this was no exception. In this instance, Mable needed someone to dispatch an unwanted, nuisance cat that had been loitering about their yard. As we were like the Home Hardware slogan "Neighbour helping neighbour," Mother ordered me to go and see what I could do to alleviate Mable's obvious stress. In anticipation of the worst, I grabbed my .22-calibre rifle and headed next door. When I arrived I spotted this large, grey, unassuming cat sitting at the back door. Knowing this was the problem feline, I inquired why this animal deserved an untimely termination.

Mable snapped, "He was killing the birds, so he has to be dealt with." She then went on to say that she would have to give him a good breakfast before the end.

Despite my confusion with the seemingly conflicting directions, she provided some bologna to the condemned and sat waiting for it to finish what was to be his final meal. While I was under strict orders to permit him to finish, I failed to fully understand the logic of the directive so I did what any impulsive kid would do. I waited for the right moment and I let him have it. The shot rang out, and almost immediately the back door flew open. Mable stood there and demanded to know the fate of the cat. Almost simultaneously Ernie appeared with the same question. Both of the people thanked me and sent me on my way. This was just another day on Ernie and Mable's farm.

As I walked across the field toward home that day, still trying to understand the events of the past few hours, I decided to check the few traps that I had set for groundhogs in the area. One of those traps had been tripped and was sitting obscured in a hole. I grabbed the chain and pulled with all my might. Suddenly, to my great and immediate distress, I discovered that I had ensnared a skunk, which instantly let me have it—at close range. Perhaps this was karma striking a blow for the big grey cat, but for the moment, that didn't matter much. I was in a bit of a fix.

Upon arriving home, my father, who had been feeding the pigs, stuck his head out of the door and yelled, "What the hell have you gotten yourself into?"

After a bit of a father-son dressing down, Father ordered me to head to the river for a long bath. I was also instructed to leave my clothes submerged in the river under a rock for the week. I did as I was told, but the overpowering odour still lingered for several days. Needless to say I was not particularly popular at home or at school for the duration of my affliction but I had learned a valuable life lesson. That was my one and only run-in with a skunk. From that day forward I was a little less eager to stick my hand or head into an unknown space and I made it a point to give all skunks a far wider berth. Upon reflection you could say I'd had a very bad day, but upon more balanced reflection, by comparison to the grey cat, I still counted myself lucky.

TEESWATER FAIR

Driving is a spectacular form of amnesia. Everything is to be discovered.
—Jean Baudrillard

While I was born well after the dawn of the motor car, my childhood happened during a time when large animal, such as horses, were still used for a range of on-farm, work-related applications. Despite the fact that we plowed with horses, even today when I think of vintage automobiles like the Packard, Willys-Knight, Overland and Studebaker, I am suddenly transported back to a much simpler time. For example, my first recollection of a car at home was an old Model T Ford with a cloth top, which Father bought used.

Despite the fact that the car was not new, the Model T was a family car, not a farm or work vehicle. It was something that was only driven during the nice weather and put up on blocks in storage during the winter.

When there was nice weather, my siblings and I looked at that old Model T as our personal ticket to fun and adventure. I remember taking numerous family trips in the Model T, but none were as far as the 30-mile trek to the Teeswater Fair. In the 1930s, Teeswater's Fair was the largest and most spectacular in the entire area. I remember chugging along in the car, Father at the wheel, wondering if we would ever get there. In those days, 30 miles seemed much farther than it is today, and looking back I have often wondered how my parents managed to wrangle the entire family into such a small car for such a long and difficult trip down nothing but bumpy and dusty gravel roads.

After the family Model T had had its day, Father upgraded to a used 1931 Chrysler DeSoto. In comparison to the Model T, the DeSoto was not unlike a tank. Father bought it at a farm auction for $201, which was a good deal for such a solid and quiet car. The car did have one flaw. It had a jerky clutch when starting off in high gear, something that often caused commotion among the kids in the back and even prompted an occasional adult phrase from Father in the front.

The DeSoto allowed us to dramatically expand the range of our family excursions. I remember one such trip to St. Catharines, which was, at the time, home base for our family friends, the Daymans. To put this into perspective, St. Catharines is about 142 miles from Auburn, a distance that is nearly five times the distance between home and the Teeswater Fairgrounds. By today's standards this trip might sound simple enough, but given that Father was not familiar with city driving, the trip was a journey that probably trimmed years off of each of our lives. After all, it would still be many decades before stoplights, traffic congestion and large highways would find their way into Huron County.

On one particular occasion, Herman Daer joined Father, Mother and me on the trip to the city. Herman sat in the front seat to help Father navigate and Mother and I were relegated to the back. In retrospect, I suppose Father expected that he would only have one driver in the car, but as luck would have it he actually had four.

At the time, King's Highway #8 ran directly through Hamilton (a large city directly along the route to St. Catharines), and as there were more than a few detours and several stoplights between home and the intended final destination, Father had several opportunities to benefit from the constant and often conflicting assistance of his backseat helpers. For example, at each stop Herman would yell out from the passenger's seat, "G'wan, g'wan" while at the same time Mother would shriek "stop, stop!" from the back.

That day, as we traversed the 284-mile round-trip, Father maintained his cool and collected disposition despite the jerky clutch, the unfamiliar city road rules and especially the backseat drivers' assistance that "guided" him along Highway 8 back to Blyth and on to Auburn. Needless to say, when we finally glimpsed the road sign indicating that we were once again returning to Highway #8 (which meant we were nearing familiar territory on the ride home), the occupants of the car let out a collective sigh, and simultaneously Herman exclaimed, "By the Jesus, it's good old Number 8."

After that trip, it would seem that there was a bit of a gap before our next outing. Perhaps Father needed to regain his composure with a sip of cider from the cellar.

An Apple in the Eye

I've never let my school interfere with my education.
—Mark Twain

I started my formal education at the tender age of 6 in a one-room school in East Wawanosh referred to as School Section (S.S.) 16. The modest grey-brick structure had no basement and was, in total, not more than 500 square feet. Included in that space was an anteroom, which was relatively basic and provided students with a place to hang our coats and store our boots. The room also contained a pail of fresh water and a cup for students to quench our thirst before entering one of the two doors on either side of the room. To the left was a door leading to the shelves where the girls could store their lunch pails and books, and to the right was a similar setup for the boys. These areas fed into the main classroom, which was, during the colder months, heated with a fire in a large box stove at the back.

The main classroom housed a desk for each student. The desks were arranged in rows and the older kids sat nearer to the back while the younger pupils in the class occupied the front rows. The rear door led to the woodshed and to a primitive, double-three-holed outhouse that was partitioned off to accommodate gender. While these paneled dividers were intended to promote privacy, I think it is fair to say that privacy was generally in short supply for the duration of my time at S.S. 16.

My first teacher was Alberta Richmond. Miss Richmond was fairly even-tempered and would tolerate almost anything except fighting. If you happened to be caught fighting with a classmate, Miss Richmond would march you to the anteroom where you would receive four or five good slaps on each hand with the leather strap. That is if you were lucky you would get four or five slaps. If you happened to jerk your hand away at any time, Miss Richmond would dole out double the punishment. Unfortunately, I know this from personal experience. In one particular case, Amy Toll and I got into a slight tussle, and true to form, once the teacher discovered what we had been up to we were unceremoniously marched through the class to the anteroom for our chastisement. As if the strap at school wasn't bad enough, once Father heard about my transgression, a similar home-based penalty was imposed for good measure.

Despite the harsh penalties, I can't say that I didn't deserve whatever I was given. My teachers were fair but firm and whether the punishment was being administered by Alberta Richmond, Bernice Lawson (Bernice later married my uncle Oliver Anderson) or Irene Stoll (each of these women taught me at some point in my educational tenure), the strict approach helped make me who I am today. For this, I am grateful to the entire group.

As a supplement to that group, I should also mention that there was a school inspector who would visit a couple of times per year. The inspector, a Mr. Jim Kincaid, made certain the teachers were doing their job correctly and that each student received board-mandated things such as the required vaccination for smallpox. While Mr. Kincaid was not popular for his delivery of needles, in hindsight, he was an important part of the team.

Bernice Lawson and the scholars of S.S. 16.
Bob McClinchey, upper right, back row.

Aside from actual building and the teachers, the yard was yet another important element of my childhood. In those days the schoolyard did not have fancy, safety-tested play equipment for students to occupy themselves with. Alternatively, S.S. 16 had a large apple-laden tree near the end of the outhouse. That tree was our "play equipment," and at recess the energetic and rambunctious boys would spring into the tree for what could only be described as an all-out, no-holds-barred apple fight. As silly as it sounds now, we would spend our free time sitting perched in the tree, periodically exposing our head to the opposing team member in an effort to entice that person to take his best shot. For the most part they missed their mark, but I do recall one time when a sluggish younger student took a northern spy in the eye. As if that wasn't bad enough, after the incident was reported to the teacher, all the boys in the school had to collect every apple in the yard and throw them over the fence. That single incident ended our apple wars in the yard, but it certainly didn't end our often ill-conceived games.

In addition to games such as baseball, tag and catch, which one would expect to find in any elementary schoolyard, we also played a game we referred to as "stick-up." The game was simple enough and required only the most basic of equipment. That being a large stick, sharpened to a point, and a good, strong throwing arm. Essentially it could be described as a cross between life-sized darts and competitive javelin for kids. In contrast today, schools are obsessed with safety. Playground equipment has to be tested and retested to ensure that children cannot be injured while at play. Even the ground must be swathed with a spongy and malleable covering to prevent injury in the event a child is to take a tumble. Looking back on my days hanging from trees and throwing sharpened sticks around the yard, I am left bewildered at how the world has changed in such a short amount of time. I sure consider myself lucky to have attended a place like S.S. 16.

Fire in the Belly

Some parents say it is toy guns that make boys warlike.
But give a boy a rubber duck and he will seize its neck
like the butt of a pistol and shout, "Bang!"
—George F. Will

It is not uncommon for today's newspaper headlines to talk about bullying in schools. While this is certainly not a good thing, it is an occurrence that is far from being a new phenomenon.

I know from where I speak. Even in my day there was a certain amount of bullying in the school, and unfortunately, I was at times the recipient of the unwanted attention.

I recall one specific tormenter named Elsie Shell. Elsie, who was an older girl, lived along the path between S.S. 16 and my home, which meant I needed to pass by her laneway each and every day. Elsie found school more of a challenge than I did, and I suspect I drew her ire because of this. Regardless of the reasons, Elsie enjoyed slapping me about both in school and whenever she had the chance during the walk home each day. This caused me to dread the daily trip home until one of the older boys with a bicycle, Jack Bennett, offered me a lifeline. He saw that I was dealing with a bully, so each day until Elsie's attention moved to someone else, he let me ride on the crossbar of his bike past Elsie, past her laneway and past her daily dosage of abuse. I certainly appreciated his help.

Now, inasmuch as I was myself bullied on occasion, I am reluctant to admit that I was, from time to time, the one doing the bullying. Perhaps bullying is too strong a word. Given my often mischievous and impish sense of humour, I would more accurately classify my behaviour as teasing, taunting or even as playing practical jokes—practical jokes that sometimes went wrong.

One particular Halloween night, a group of kids from the school, myself included, got together and decided to play a trick on Davey Gwynn. Davey was an area character who was hired by the school section trustees to light a fire in the classroom stove each morning when needed. Davey typically lit the box stove at the back of the classroom early in the morning so that the building was warmed sufficiently by the time the teacher and students arrived for 9:00 a.m. classes. Our so-called plan was simple enough, but to a group of children looking to stir up trouble, it seemed funny and clever at the time.

We managed to break into the school and crammed the old stove with at least three tiers of hardwood—materials that Davey would need to remove prior to lighting the stove for the day. At best this would cause him a bit of extra time, but we thought the caper was hilarious; at least we did at first. Additionally, to add insult to injury, we also placed the teacher's desk atop the stove for good measure.

The morning after we had launched our plan, the Toll family, who lived next to the school, noticed a heat haze above the roof of S.S. 16. They rushed over to the school to investigate the discovery and found the building ablaze. It seems that the stove, still hot from the previous day's fire, had ignited the hardwood we had piled on top of the embers. The subsequent fire burned so hot that it melted the stove and burnt the floor through. The entire stove then dropped into the dugout below the classroom, and that was when the sparks really started to fly. It is also worth mentioning that, as a result of the unfortunate new placement of the teacher's desk, all of her books, personal items and school records were destroyed in the blaze.

Following the fire, many of the parents from the area called for a new school to be built in place of the heavily damaged structure. Other, more fiscally conservative neighbours suggested repairing the existing building. While the latter of the two options eventually won out, the decision only occurred after an investigation of the cause was completed. As you might expect, it didn't take long for the investigators to figure out what had actually happened. Once the cause had been revealed, it took even less time for the young culprits to be collared. My friends and I were individually called in and vigorously questioned by the insurance company. I guess our respective stories checked out, because rather than throw us in the clink, the powers that be put us to work for weeks manually scraping and completely repainting the entire inside of the school.

At the same time as I was paying my debt to society, I was dealing with serious repercussions at home. Needless to say, my father was not impressed by my antics, but this was not to be the last time he and I would clash over my approach and thoughts as they related to school.

After completing my time at S.S. 16, I moved on to a continuation school in Auburn. Subsequent to that I entered Goderich District Collegiate Institute (GDCI) for the balance of my school days, a term that was unexpectedly cut short one day while I was in grade 11. That was the day I had decided to cut class in favour of an afternoon at Wood's Pool Room. That was the first and the last time I would ever cut class, but that single event would prove to be a seminal event in my young life.

So there I was, enjoying my afternoon at the pool hall in Goderich when, to my absolute astonishment and horror, in walks my father. He headed straight over to me, and in no uncertain terms declared that if I wasn't going to go to school faithfully then I would need to get a real job. Up to this point in my life I had only held part-time jobs as a general farm labourer and a pin-boy at the local bowling alley (something that paid about 15 cents per game). Obviously the prospect of permanently leaving school and getting a real job was a shock that I had not planned for when I woke up that morning, but Father was undeniably serious. As a result, at the age of 15 I was nudged to take my first steps into the world of work. Little did I know the adventure that I was now being set on.

FOWL TEMPERED

My mother said I must always be intolerant of ignorance but
understanding of illiteracy. That some people, unable to go to school,
were more educated and more intelligent than college professors.
—Maya Angelou

For me, school was always a necessary evil. Most days I would have preferred to pursue other, more enjoyable things, such as fishing or swimming in the river. Despite my own proclivities, Mother made it clear that a proper education was something that was going to happen whether I approved or not. Notwithstanding this parentally imposed love of classroom learning, my elementary school days were still a time that afforded me with numerous opportunities to learn much more than what could be found on the blackboard at school.

More often than not, these "opportunities" took the form of relationships and extracurricular interaction with colourful characters from the area. One such character was unquestionably a man by the name of Davey Gwynn. Davey and his family lived in a rather "rustic" house on the "wild hundred," which was owned at the time by Fred Toll. In addition to being a veteran of the First World War, Davey was hired by the school section trustees to light a fire in the classroom stove each morning that it was needed. I suppose that was how I first met Davey.

Davey, who was much older than I, was married to a neighbour woman named Jessie McCullough. The duo was arguably an odd match, but together they raised a family of five boys and a girl. Their daughter, Helena, attended the public elementary school while I was there, a second connection between Davey and me.

As far as I could tell, the family existed in a fairly rough environment. Davey primarily supported the family with odd jobs and whatever he could scrounge off the land. Suffice it to say, hunting, fishing and trapping were the primary staples, supplemented only by an occasional day's work offered by a neighbour, family member or an area business looking for a capable manual labourer.

Most people knew Davey was willing to do just about anything to make ends meet, so he often was the one tasked with the difficult and dirty jobs that others didn't want. As one example of the lengths to which Davey would go to generate income, I remember that he used to skin skunks and a range of other animals for their hides. This practice was normal enough in those days, with one notable exception. Davey did both his skinning and fat rendering in the house. The kitchen stove served as the tanking location, turning out lard, tallow and a rather distinctive and pungent smell that lingered constantly in the Gwynn household.

Davey may have been a good worker but he was no textbook academic. As the story goes, when Fred Toll was first negotiating rental terms with Davey, Fred suggested a yearly price of $60, a fee that included unlimited firewood at no extra cost. The proposal apparently riled the often brusque Davey, who responded that there was no damn way that he was going to pay $60 per year for the house. Davey immediately countered the offer by saying that he would be prepared to pay not one cent more than $5 per month; that was his final offer. Fred smirked, shook his head and agreed without further discussion.

Despite Davey's obvious challenges with basic arithmetic, he was a man with common street-smarts. As one inventive way to supplement the family income, Davey turned those street-smarts into a budding yet successful home-based business. In those days, Huron County was a dry county; at least the areas not immediately surrounding Davey's house were dry. In an effort to make some extra money by using his unique skill set, Davey Gwynn started bootlegging beer. To avoid police detection, Davey kept the beer in a cold spring some distance from his house. Customers seeking a sip of his skunky brew were required to sound their car horn several times before making the covert pick-up on a side road near the property. Once the customer sounded the horn and was in the correct position, Davey would come running out of the bush with a basket full of mud-covered bottles. His fee for this home grown vintage was 30 cents per bottle. He also ran a periodic special of three bottles for one dollar, but it was not the kind of special that generated too much interest for customers. Again, Davey's lacklustre mathematic abilities were not quite as honed as his work ethic.

With all the business activities in and around the Gwynn house, the location quickly earned itself the less-than-flattering handle "Wild Cat Inn." The Wild Cat Inn was certainly renowned for its beer-like brew but it was much less sought-after for its cuisine. On one particular occasion, a friend of mine took a traveller to the Wild Cat Inn for a beverage. Once there, the traveller asked Jessie if he could have a sandwich to accompany his bootlegged beer. She agreed and immediately sent her son Fergus into the pantry to retrieve the cheese and the other elements of a sandwich. Just as Fergus disappeared into the pantry, a flurry of feathers, squawks and screams erupted. Fergus exploded back into the kitchen, followed quickly by an ornery and territorial old rooster that had taken up temporary residence in the storeroom. A surprised and slightly shaken Fergus timidly announced to the entire room that the idea of sandwiches would need to be reconsidered as the resident poultry had eaten all the cheese. The patrons were generally unconcerned with the development as their appetites had already flown the coop with the foul-tempered fowl.

STOMPIN' BOB

All things are difficult before they are easy.
—Thomas Fuller

At the age of 15 I found myself out of school and looking for full-time work for the first time in my young life. With the benefit of hindsight, in many ways the moment when Father found me skipping school in Wood's Pool Room and subsequently thrust me into the working world was a blessing of sorts. While that confrontation certainly strained my adult relationship with my father, it effectively set me down a path that was to be one of the defining moments of my life. While I may not have grasped it at the time, that moment in a Goderich Pool Hall helped make me that jack of all trades I would eventually become

I was 15, green and didn't necessarily have any special skills or abilities. Despite the predicament, I was unattached, eager to learn, prepared to work and armed with a strong and unswerving sense of humour. As the saying goes, the world was my oyster and I was ready to start shucking.

One autumn in particular, a friend and I hitchhiked the 88 miles from Auburn to Tillsonburg, Ontario. We didn't really have a plan but hoped we might find work helping with the tobacco harvest. Tobacco was big business to Tillsonburg, and due to the labour-intensive harvesting process, was a tremendous employer for young men who were not afraid to get their hands dirty (little did we know just how dirty our hands would soon be). All of this, mixed with the journey to Tillsonburg itself, certainly appealed to my sense of adventure.

For the uninitiated, tobacco is cultivated similarly to many other agricultural products grown in the southern Ontario region. Seeds are planted, and once the plants are about eight inches tall, they are transplanted into the fields. Years ago, the transplanting process was quite arduous and reliant upon specific timing. Tobacco farmers used to have to wait for rainy weather to soften the ground before planting could start. Once the weather and the soil were ready, a hole was created in the tilled earth with something called a tobacco peg. In those days, a tobacco peg was either a curved wooden tool or a deer antler. After you made two holes to the right and left, you would then move forward two feet, select plants from your bag and repeat the entire process. Much of this is today done with machines, but the priming and harvesting remains the most difficult and labour-intensive parts of the process.

Tobacco can be harvested in many ways, but the oldest method, still commonly used today, sees the entire plant harvested by cutting off the stalk at the ground with a tobacco knife. The severed plant is then speared onto sticks and hung in a curing barn. Other, better-quality tobacco is harvested by fieldworkers who select only the bottom leaves (so-called "sand leaves") as they ripen. Again, only the lower, prime-quality leaves are picked at any one time. As time passes and the other leaves ripen, they too become prime. As a result, "primers" get to go through the field again and again, earning more money with each pass.

Of course we didn't know any of this prior to our arrival in Tillsonburg. Shortly following our arrival I was hired as a primer on a tobacco farm near the unincorporated community of Glen Meyer. Glen Meyer is nestled in Norfolk County, immediately southeast of Tillsonburg. I was astonished to be offered a whopping $7.00 per day for my services. The going rate for labour at home in Huron County was a meagre $1.50 per day, so this was a huge step up. I remember thinking that, if all went according to my plan, I could have some serious money socked away in a very short amount of time. But this joy quickly wore thin as my first week priming tobacco started to unfold. As you might expect, this constant cutting, tying and hanging is backbreaking and dirty work. Your hands and clothes quickly become covered with sticky tar and your back aches constantly from leaning and lifting. You also have to remember that this was all being done in the blistering sun.

Put another way, priming tobacco was some of the most gruelling work of my life.

There were six of us working as primers and our workday usually began just ahead of 7:00 a.m. Once the horse was ready, the basic plan for the day was for the six of us to prime enough tobacco to fill the drying kiln (also known as a curing barn) for the evening run. We always started from the bottom of the plant, which meant that we had to work under the upper leaves. As a result, after the first few armfuls of leaves had been carried to the boat, our clothes were soaked with the morning dew that had settled overnight on the plants. Worse still, as the day progressed the wet dew was replaced with sticky and smelly tar residue. We often joked that our clothes would be so covered with tobacco tar that at the end of the day, we would just stand our pants up in the corner so we could use them the next morning.

Once the horse-drawn boat was loaded, we would run the horse to the kiln, where other workers would unload and tie the tobacco leaves onto sticks long enough to hang on the rafters in the kiln. As I recall, the kiln would hold somewhere in the neighbourhood of about 1400 loaded sticks and it needed to be filled each afternoon. As primers, our job had to be wrapped up by four o'clock each afternoon to give the other workers the time they needed to prepare the kiln. After that, the entire process started over again the next morning.

Another difficult job associated with the tobacco harvest was "suckering." Suckering was yet another backbreaking, dirty and miserable job called for on that Glen Meyer farm. While it was certainly necessary, I believe it would be fair to suggest that suckering tobacco was probably the most hated of all tobacco-growing jobs. In the simplest of terms, suckering involved removing tender sprouts at each junction of leaf and stalk. Removing the suckers strengthened the plant, encouraged the development of the body and improved the overall quality of the leaves. I dreaded suckering because it required the pulling of thousands of suckers from the stalks at a time when the tobacco was growing rapidly and oozing tar. Though not immediately visible, the stuff seemed to drip from nearly every part of the plant. The sticky substance would build up on any surface that came in contact with the plant. After working in the fields for even a short time, your hands, shirts, arm hair and even your eyebrows would be covered with a thick film of the dark sticky stuff. After a day of suckering, you could easily spend another day washing, pulling and scraping tar from your clothes and skin.

The harvest could take six to eight weeks to complete depending on the size of the acreage, but a good worker could bring home as much as $50 per week. I was in Tillsonburg to make my fortune, and when you consider the economics of the day, this was tremendous money that I was all too happy to get.

In 1971 Stompin' Tom Connors released his hit song "Tillsonburg." The song, which told the painful tale of how Charles Thomas Connors worked in the tobacco fields during his youth, reached the 12th spot on the Canadian Music Charts, but after my personal experiences in the tobacco fields of southern Ontario, the song was number one with me.

The War at Home

God gives every bird its food, but he does not throw it into its nest.
—J. G. Holland

On September 1, 1939, Germany invaded Poland, and with that one act of aggression the world's great military powers were thrust into what would come to be known as the war to end all wars. With the eventual global declaration of war, the world's great military powers engaged and began revving their economies in an attempt to support and bolster their respective war efforts. Factories started to run extra shifts, female workers were hired to replace deploying men and governments flung open their national treasuries in an effort to grow their manufacturing and labour capacities as fast and as far as possible.

Obviously the war was one of the darkest periods in human history, but it was also a time of nearly endless employment opportunities for young, able-bodied men. In particular, tradesmen were in tremendous demand across Canada and much of the world. For me this meant a brief return to the classroom. This time, I travelled to Kitchener, where I enrolled in a machine-shop course. It seems to me the entire course took about 30 days to complete, but once I was finished, I had a ticket to my next great adventure.

Armed with my new certificate as a machinist and my thumb for hitching a ride, I threw my hat over the wall and headed for the home of a family friend who lived in St. Catharines. Bob Dayman was someone I first met through my father many years earlier, and as luck would have it, he lived near Welland, Ontario, a place where I had heard jobs were plentiful. True to form, Bob drove me to Welland, where I managed to pick up a job at Atlas Steel. Atlas Steel was, at the time, a plant that had been drafted by the military to produce steel products for the allies. While it promised to pay the bills, it was dirty, loud and miserable work that I didn't much care for. I tried it for a few days but quickly realized that Atlas Steel was not the gig for me.

I made the move down the road to Commonwealth Electric, an upstart company that had arrived in the community just a few years earlier, in 1936. I enjoyed the work at Commonwealth Electric much better but I also enjoyed the fact that I didn't have to uproot and move yet again. When I first moved to town I found a small but comfortable room in a local boarding house beside the Welland Canal. I didn't have a television but I found that I really enjoyed watching the operations of the canal. Somehow watching the bridges moving up and down to accommodate the passing freighters was oddly rhythmic or even therapeutic. It may have been a simple thing but it helped Welland feel more like home during my stay in the area.

After a couple of months in my adopted, albeit temporary home on the canal, I was made aware that the Dominion Road Machinery Company in Goderich was looking for qualified employees. Goderich was just a few short miles from my childhood home so I eagerly jumped at the chance to return to Huron County. With my experiences as a machinist, I was quickly hired at Dominion Roads, where I spent the next year as an operator on a number of machines within the factory. I actually liked my time at Dominion Roads; most particularly I was fond of working on the lathe, something I became quite good at. On the whole, I enjoyed working in a drier, cleaner and more home-based environment, but once the warm spring and summer months rolled around, I found that I started to long for outdoor work again. Perhaps I was harkening back to my formative years working on the farm, but outdoor work seemed to be in my blood. I may have mentioned this notion to a few of my friends because word apparently got out, and one night the plant foreman approached me with a rather stern look on his face. His name was Mr. A. McDonald, and he was someone who didn't hold back.

He marched up to me and said, "I hear you're wanting to quit." I confirmed that I had in fact been thinking about my departure, to which he fired back, "I just came by to tell you that you can't quit, so you'd better get used to picking shit with the rest of us here."

Of course he was referring to the fact that there was a national shortage of skilled tradesmen, and given that the war effort was still in full swing, quitting was not as easy as it may have sounded. Little did he know that the farm labour shortage outweighed other labour shortages by a country mile.

The next morning I visited Selective Services and told them I needed to quit so I could return to work on the family farm. They agreed that agriculture had a higher priority than manufacturing so I was given permission to serve my notice. Two weeks later my tenure at the Dominion Road Machinery Company in Goderich came to an end and I signed up for a harvest excursion headed west.

Memories and Milford's Tow

As soon as the harvest is in, you're a migrant
worker. Afterward just a bum.
—Nunnally Johnson

I was 17 years old in 1943 when Andy Plunkett, Joe Hunking and I boarded the train bound for Saskatoon as part of a harvest excursion. A harvest excursion was a common practice in western Canada in the late nineteenth and early twentieth centuries, where a large numbers of workers from eastern Canada and the British Isles would travel to the Canadian West to participate in the annual fall harvest. At the time there were severe labour shortages on the prairies and these shortages became most extreme during the months of September and October, when millions of acres of crops needed to be harvested. This traditional labour problem was exacerbated by the fact that Canada had sent thousands of young, able-bodied men to the front lines as part of the war effort. Irrespective of WWII, Canadian wheat needed to be harvested and a shortage of workers could not be permitted to stand in the way.

With this in mind, beginning in 1890, harvest excursions were organized by the Canadian Pacific Railway (CPR). Each fall, CPR would organize special trains which would, for approximately $30, transport a worker from central Canada to various agricultural centres on the prairies. The labourers were given low fares by the CPR as the railway knew they would later earn a great deal of profit from transporting the harvest yields to eastern ports. From my perspective at the time, wages were high, the highest a labourer could earn anywhere in Canada. A season's work could put as much as $300 in my pocket, and despite the horrid condition on the trains, I wasn't about to miss out on an opportunity like that.

After three days and nights on a cramped and dirty train, Andy, Joe and I arrived in Saskatoon, Saskatchewan. After arriving we headed north to an area near the village of Laird and the slightly larger town of Rosthern. Milford and Elsie Doerr, relatives of mine, lived near Laird so we headed their way. Soon after arriving we each accepted a job with a local threshing crew. The days were long and difficult but the outside physical work was what I really wanted to be doing. The three of us worked together, but I was the one assigned the job of driving the team of horses (hauling the "sheaves" or "bundles" as they were commonly called).

Our day usually started at 5:00 a.m. The horses need to be fed, watered and harnessed before the 6:00 a.m. breakfast bell sounded. After that we were off to the threshing site to start the day's work. The women would generally bring us a hearty lunch at 9:00 a.m., at noon and again at 3:00 p.m. each day. Then we would work until around 7:00 p.m. when we would again be presented with a meal, our fifth and last of the day. There was no question that the work was hard and quite physical but I don't ever remember being hungry on the job. Unlike some of my previous vocations, I worked at this one until the harvest was finished. Looking back on that summer, I wonder if it reminded me of living and working on the home farm. In any event, farm work was something I enjoyed for a large portion of my life.

Once the threshing was done, I soon moved on to other similar opportunities on the prairies. One such opportunity even gave me the chance to leap into the so-called modern farming era.

In 1932 the International Harvester Company produced their first diesel engine and they set it in a bulldozer-like machine called a McCormick-Deering TD-40 Crawler (it had tracks rather than wheels). This engine was unique in that it started on gasoline and then switched over to diesel fuel. As with diesel engines today, the extra power is useful when you need muscle on the farm, but the first diesel engines were difficult to start in cold weather. This was a serious failing in the prairie climate, so the Crawler was a major innovation. Using gasoline allowed the engine to start easily and thoroughly warm up before making the switch to diesel in all weather conditions. Then, in 1935, this engine was put in the International Harvester WD-40, becoming the first diesel tractor on wheels in North America. The WD-40 was the beast that I first used for mechanized farm work. I remember pulling 17 feet of one-way discs. It was slow and laborious and took about one hour to harrow one round, but it was the modern age and I loved it.

By this time Joe Hunking was quite homesick so he packed his bags and headed back east. Andy and I opted to stay in Saskatchewan for the duration so we headed to my cousin's farm about four miles outside of Laird. Milford and Elsie hosted us until Christmas, and during our stay, we helped around the farm. They had a few cows that needed to be milked, and just for good measure, the first one done milking had to fill the cream separator. The separator was in the kitchen, so milk had to be carried in buckets and dumped into it.

One fateful morning I was the lucky one tasked with the separator job. I filled the tub, grabbed the crank and started turning the gears. Suddenly and without warning I learned one important detail. The cream separator wasn't bolted to the floor. In my haste to start the job, I upset the entire machine and the gallons of milk waiting to be separated. Of course this caused quite the commotion among the 12 or so members of the feline population that had been sitting in wait for just such an accident. Needless to say they got their fill that morning as I scrambled to clean up the mess before anyone else caught wind of it.

Milford and Elsie were good people. They worked hard and treated us right. Often, after the work was done, Milford and I would sit and listen to some old-time music on the radio. Again, perhaps it prompted memories of home, but it was something I really looked forward to.

I also looked forward to Andy's pranks, his favourite of which was to go outside and "adjust" the radio antennas. Once the antenna was pointed in the new direction, if you listened closely you could usually hear the swearing from within the house as the listeners slapped the sides of their radios in a frantic attempt to restore the favourite programs. If they had ever known we were responsible for the disruption, there would have been a lot more static than was on the radio.

My time is Saskatchewan was also my first lesson in driving on "gumbo." This was long before pavement was common, and the roads around Laird were composed mostly of clay (or at least a clay-like substance). As you can imagine, for the uninitiated, clay is not especially easy to manoeuvre when it is wet or covered in snow. One night I offered to drive Elsie to one of her meetings in town. It was only about four miles away, but once we arrived it started to rain quite heavily. Eventually the meeting wrapped up and about 11:00 p.m. we headed for home.

It seemed like we had just passed the town limits when I hit a patch of this gumbo, and, like Bambi on ice, I spun out of control, finally coming to rest in a stubble field just off the highway. Not one to give up easily, I spent the next several minutes spinning and rocking the car in an effort to break free or to at least gain some ground on the road to home. Unfortunately, after hitting what we called a "slew," which was nothing more than a wet hole in the field, my fate was sealed. At that point, being the gentleman that I am, I walked the remaining three miles home and rousted Milford from what I assumed was a peaceful and pleasant sleep. He was predictably pleased with the story and even more so with the prospect of having to pull us out in the middle of the night using his tractor with spade lugs. Needless to say, it took quite a while for me to live that one down.

Not long after that, Andy and I headed for home and we didn't see Milford or Elsie again until they sold their farm in Laird and moved to Ontario. They moved east to Zurich where they purchased and operated a successful general store business for many years, and while I am certain they missed their comfortable home on the outskirts of Laird, I was at least able to see more of them when they lived in Zurich.

EIGHTEEN WHEELS ... OF CHEESE

I got a job immediately after leaving high school; I was lucky—three dollars a week and all I could eat, working on a vegetable truck.

—Ernest Borgnine

After returning to Ontario from my harvest excursion, I picked up a few odd jobs on farms in and around the Blyth and Auburn areas. Then, the following spring a cheese cooperative sprang up in Blyth. The manager of the newly minted co-op was Carman Hodgins who, despite my slight driving mishap on the gumbo-based roads of Saskatchewan, hired me to drive truck and help make cheese. I worked under the tutelage of Jim Laurie, who made the cheese, and Walter Buttle, who was responsible for firing the boiler. My job was essentially to help Jim and Walter with whatever they needed.

As an aside, working with Jim and Walter was an enjoyable employment sentence to say the least. The two were both, in their own right, great entertainers at concerts and other community events and festivals. Additionally, the duo never missed an opportunity to showcase their highly developed and finely accomplished talents for singing, harmonizing and, more often than not, cracking jokes or playing pranks on whoever happened to be the closest. It is worth noting that their unique brand of practical humour wasn't above self-deprecation when the occasion presented itself. In one such case, I once quizzed Walter, who was a very small man, on why he was so short and slight. In response, without missing a beat, Walter declared for all within ear-shot that, "I was born the smallest of triplets, and to make matters worse, my two brothers got to suckle Ma and I was forced to suckle Pa." Needless to say, I avoided the subject in the future.

Now, making cheese was an interesting process and the company at the co-op was good, but my interests remained behind a wheel that was not made of cheese. Fortunately, a few weeks later, George Charter approached me about driving truck for him. George had a Dodge tractor and a 26-foot trailer, which was the biggest rig in the area at the time. From a career perspective, the offer seemed like a step in the right direction so I hit the open road. Just imagine, in a span of fewer than 10 years I went from being a farm kid who never travelled more than a few miles from home to a man who was driving both long- and short-haul for a living. This was going to be the life.

Here I stand with one of George Charter's trucks loaded with grape stakes destined for the Niagara region.

In the weeks and months that followed, I hauled telephone and hydro poles, grape stakes and lumber in and out of countless communities in the Niagara Region, North Bay, Trout Creek, Burkes Falls and South River, to name only a few of the places I rolled through.

As an interesting aside, in January of 1948, during my time driving for George Charter, a gallon of #2 gas sold for just 34¢. Looking back, I know that times were much leaner then, but costs were also much lower than those faced by business owners today. I was just a driver in those days, but during my years in business for myself I often marvelled at how things have changed so much in such a short time.

Gas and oil were so much cheaper in those days.

Earlier I mentioned my slight driving mishap on the "gumbo"-based roads of Saskatchewan. This was obviously an embarrassing chapter in my life, which I typically hesitate to bring up again. That said, on one trip up north for lumber, my brother Bill decided to join me for company and conversation on the ride. The outbound portion of the trip was generally quiet and uneventful but the situation on the return portion was not quite so. Just as we neared Alliston, Ontario, I must have hit some of that Saskatchewan gumbo because I rolled the truck down a steep ditch. The truck rolled over and spilled the lumber, not to mention Bill. Once the dust had settled, I looked over and noticed that Bill was lying out beside the truck, apparently half asleep. Fortunately our guardian angels were on duty that night, so neither of us was hurt. At that point, we unloaded the lumber, which George later sold to someone from the pile in the ditch, and drove the slightly damaged truck home. Needless to say, this episode brought my career driving trucks for George Charter to a screeching, immediate and unceremonious halt.

My truck had seen better days after a small mishap in a ditch near Allison. My brother Bill and Stewart Johnston take a break from unloading the cargo.

Despite the mishap, as a personal aside, some of the lumber that I hauled in those days was used to construct the first part of Bainton's Old Mill in Blyth, and after that I transported tanning machinery from Millbrook to Blyth for use by the same local family-owned business. That business, which still operates on Westmoreland Street in Blyth, later expanded and became an important industry in the community. Today as I walk up and down the streets in Blyth, I often encounter people who profess to be builders of this community, and to them I tip my hat, but then I smile. I don't hail from a wealthy family and did not go far in school, but in a very literal way I helped build—one piece of lumber at a time—the community in which I now live.

My Door Was Always Open

A career is wonderful, but you can't curl up with it on a cold night.
—Marilyn Monroe

WWII was now over, the economy was still hot and despite my previous "gumbo"-related mishap behind the wheel, Bob Henry took me on as one of his truck drivers. He had a brand new 1946 Dodge and a K6 International (a truck), and as luck would have it, he could only drive one of them at a time. To fill the obvious gap, I was hired to truck up north hauling logs out of Algonquin Park to Huntsville. I drove the Dodge, which, to accomplish the job, had been fitted with "dollies," an extra set of wheels located behind the drive wheels to help support heavier-than-usual loads.

Hauling logs in Algonquin Park was cold work.

As part of the job, it was not unheard of for Bob and me to stop over for the night in a very cold and frosty Huntsville. During the winter months, it was not out of the ordinary for Huntsville's temperatures to send the mercury to 35 or 40 degrees below zero. As if this wasn't bad enough, we typically stayed in small, temporarily constructed wooden rooms, which did the trick, except I also remember several sleepless nights because of the frost contraction of the planks. In the quiet of the night, the contractions sounded much the same as shotgun blasts being discharged. Even though we both knew what the sounds were, they were still disconcerting and almost impossible to ignore as we tried to sleep. Between the bitter cold and the constant ringing out of explosive noises, sleep was not something I did a lot of between 1946 and 1947.

The cold played havoc with more than just Bob and me. Inasmuch as we were slow to get up and moving each morning, our trucks were even more sluggish. Each day we needed to have our trucks towed before they would start. Then, once they were running and warm, the real adventure began. We were hauling for between 35 and 40 miles per load, and for three of those miles we were running over lakes. This was a new experience for me, and given my past luck on the road, I was eager to listen to the counsel of others. Bob and I were told by more seasoned ice-road truckers that the optimum speed running over ice when loaded was only 15 miles per hour. Experience taught that any slower would allow you to settle through the ice while a faster rate of speed would create a larger than normal water wave ahead of the truck, which could potentially crack, break or damage the ice in front of the truck. As both of these possibilities presented real problems for any trucker, I was careful to keep the throttle at 15 miles per hour. We were also told to make certain that the door was open whenever we were on the ice. This precaution would apparently prevent the ice and water from trapping a driver in the cab should the truck drop into the water. I'm not sure I believed that this made me any safer but believe me, my door was always open. As if all of this wasn't bad enough, sometimes the truck would lean if the track was a bit weaker or deeper on one side or the other. This, coupled with the loud cracking of the ice, especially during the first run of the day, was nerve-wracking at best. I was always happy to get all four wheels off the ice and back on solid ground.

Not everyone made it over the ice.

On a few occasions when we couldn't make it back to Huntsville for the night, we would bunk at a lumber camp. The bunkhouse didn't crack like the shacks in Huntsville did, but there were other troublesome noises and detractions that were no less disruptive to a restful sleep. Imagine 50 loggers sleeping in a single structure after working for a few weeks in the bush. Between the coughing, snoring and farting, morning could not come soon enough.

After the winter run we headed home to southern Ontario. Bob asked me if I had any interest in buying the Dodge and working for myself during the off-season. I had never really considered it, but once asked the idea took root. Later, when I was finally able to scrape together enough money, I bought the rig. For the first time in my life I was my own boss, and as my first act as a freelance trucker, I landed a contract hauling logs and lumber for Ratz Sawmill Co.

Finally it was my name on the truck door.

The company was owned by Lloyd Ratz, who had mills in both Wingham and St. Clements, Ontario. They also had a cookhouse and bunkhouse combination on the sawmill property where I stayed. If memory serves, there were about 50 men who worked and slept there at alternating and differing times.

Lloyd Ratz.

Put another way, this was not a small setup. There was a cook named Mrs. Wells and a "head sawyer" (the worker in charge of the others sawing lumber in a saw mill) named Levi Bauman who was assisted primarily by his son, Joe. Levi and Joe had a trained and experienced bush crew that cut, skidded and loaded most of the logs. The bush foreman, who ran a Caterpillar Tractor, was Oscar Tiedie. This group was augmented by the two K7 International log trucks owned internally by Ratz and driven by Ross Jamieson and Jack Harcourt. The operation was efficient and they needed to keep the logs flowing out of the bush.

Loading logs was not always as easy as it is today.

To accomplish this they hired private log trucks and drivers as needed.

Unloading lumber at the mill in Fergus.

I hauled logs and lumber to the Wingham Sawmill and to McLary's factory in Fergus nearly every day for almost two years, and in that time I learned a great deal about the business. I watched Lloyd Ratz scaling lumber while boarding a truck that to me looked pretty easy. In a nutshell, to do the job correctly you had to figure out how many board feet of Select Number One Common, Number Two Common and so on could be found in each load. You also had to record and track your numbers through a system of dots in a book. Most importantly, the process needed to be done quickly and accurately. Mistakes cost money, and that was unacceptable to any logger.

One day I mentioned that I might like to expand my duties to include taking a crack at this scaling process. Lloyd was receptive to the notion but needed to make sure I knew what I was doing. To help with this, he sent me to see Fred Pedwell in the community of Ardoch. Ardoch, which is located in North Frontenac Township just outside Ottawa, is an area that boasts a considerable amount of experience and expertise in forestry and logging. I spent two weeks in Ardoch working to board and scale lumber. It was easy enough work but I was never actually told if I was doing a good job or not. With all of this in mind, it didn't take the full two weeks for me to determine that this was not the job for me.

Miss Frances

You can discover more about a person in an hour
of play than in a year of conversation.
—Plato

As has been said in movies, books and on countless stages, "All work and no play makes Jack a dull boy." While work has been an important part of my life, my most memorable and life-altering moments have often sprouted as a result of fun and play. Perhaps the most important and memorable of these play-induced moments began when I attended a dance in the late 1940s at the Blyth Hall.

I was enjoying the music, tapping my foot, watching the crowd and generally soaking up a relaxing night on the town when suddenly, I noticed a girl. Now the room was full of young and attractive girls, but this particular girl was one of the prettiest I had ever set eyes on. I was far from bold when it came to the ladies but I had to act. I eventually worked up the confidence to go over and talk to her. I asked her to dance with me and even went so far as to offer her a ride home but she refused outright. I suspect I was deeply smitten so I was not prepared to accept her first refusal. I needed to try again so I waited until the dance ended. After that I approached the girl, who was walking home with two of her friends. I restated my offer of a ride and this time she quietly accepted.

That night I gave her a ride home and that single car ride started what was to become a lifelong ride with the love of my life.

The girl's name was Frances Hollyman, the daughter of a local businessman and a member of a well-known Blyth-based family.

Relaxing with Miss Frances.

We dated for some time, and with each passing date I was more and more certain she was the one for me. At one point, I even paid to have a professional sign painter put "Miss Frances" on the front of my truck; surely this was the ultimate signal that any young man could send to his girl.

Sometime after we first met, Fran's sister, Dorothy, and Dorothy's husband, Doug Stewart, purchased a number of small cabins at Wasaga Beach. Wasaga Beach is a small Ontario town located in Simcoe County, at the southern end of Georgian Bay.

Our cottages in Wasaga Beach.

Fran took to spending her summers there, helping take care of the cabins and selling tickets to the outdoor theatre. Of course I had little choice but to follow her north to Wasaga Beach. I spent nearly every weekend there so I put quite a few miles on my 1947 Plymouth convertible. That was a great car that allowed Frances and me to travel and explore the area.

1947: Memorable moments at Wasaga Beach.

Looking back, those days with Frances were some of the best and most carefree of our entire lives. Sure we had other good time in our nearly six decades together, but these were the days when we were first getting to know each other. These were the days when we first fell in love.

Building the foundation for a lifetime of memories.

During the summer of 1948, I took the leap and proposed to Frances—only this time when I asked her a question, she didn't refuse.

SETTING THE DATE AND THE COURSE

A successful marriage requires falling in love many times, always with the same person.
—Mignon McLaughlin

With the particulars of the formal wedding proposal now behind us, Frances, her sister and their mother, Mary, began the process of planning for the actual wedding day. Frances, who was born on July 9, 1930, was 18 years old at this point. She was not the first in her family to be married as her 33-year-old sister, Dorothy (born on June 13, 1915), had married Doug Stewart some years earlier. As far as I could see, the fact that Fran was not the first Hollyman wedding didn't seem to dampen or diminish the excitement within the household. There was going to be a wedding, and in those days, much like today, weddings were important family and social events.

Family was important. Here is a young Frances with her cousin Patricia Harrington (the future Patsy Kelso).

From a family history perspective, Fran's father, Francis John Hollyman, was born in Wales, England, on November 30, 1891. He immigrated to Canada in 1910 and just three years later in 1913, Francis married Mary Ellen Carter, a local girl born in nearby East Wawanosh Township. The couple had two daughters, and in 1927 the family set up a small bake shop on Queen Street in Blyth.

Hollyman's Bakery in Blyth.

In much the same way as I worked with my father on the family farm, Frances worked for her dad delivering bread by horse and cart to the houses and farms in and around the Londesboro area.

Hollyman's delivery cart—Fran's "mobile office."

That would have been back in the early 1940s, and Frances often regaled that a loaf of freshly baked, hand-delivered Hollyman bread retailed for about eight cents each. As cheap as that sounds today, she also noted that the five-cent, day-old bread sold faster still; I suppose everyone loves a deal. The Hollyman family operated their bakery until 1944, when they sold the business to Frank Wasman. After several years of retirement, Francis John Hollyman died at his home in Blyth on October 5, 1956. His wife, Mary, survived him until May 2, 1964, when she too passed.

All this to say, the Hollyman family was made up of good, civically minded, hardworking people that I was lucky to meet and even luckier to get to know well. With this as a backdrop, after Frances and I dated for a couple of years, we set the date for the wedding. We said our vows on May 27, 1950, at the Hollyman home in Blyth, under the watchful eye of Reverend Rogers, as our friends and families looked on. Following the ceremony we spent a few days on our honeymoon travelling to the Niagara region. We crossed the Canada/US border at Buffalo, passed through Cleveland and headed for home via Detroit.

I was finally married to my soul mate.
Father, Mother, me, Fran, Mary and Frank Hollyman on the big day.

I should mention that, for our honeymoon, I had a nice 1947 Pontiac Straight 8. Not too long after we completed our honeymoon I made a decision to trade that car for something more modest. Fran always quipped that I kept the car just long enough to get her and then I sold it. We both loved that car.

Here I am with the car both Fran and I loved.

That said, upon our arrival home to Blyth, Fran's parents approached us with a potential career option. This time it was neither ice-road trucking nor delivering bread on a horse-drawn cart. This time there was a general store for sale in Ruthven, a hamlet of fewer than 400 residents in the rural Ontario Township of Kingsville. We wanted to settle down as a married couple, and Frank and Mary wondered if Frances and I would be interested in a partnership of sorts. As a newly married and out-of-work young couple, we had nothing to lose.

We operated that store (known then as the Hollyman & McClinchey General Store) for a couple of months, but despite frugal bookkeeping, our collective business acumen and copious amounts of sweat equity, the store was simply not as lucrative as we might have hoped or needed. Fortunately, two months into our ill-conceived business venture, another couple wandered into the store and asked if we would consider selling the entire operation to them. As you might expect, we could hardly sign the papers fast enough and almost before the ink was dry, we were loaded into my 1947 Straight 8 Pontiac and headed back to Blyth.

Here I am standing outside of the Hollyman & McClinchey
General Store in Ruthven.

After our stint in Ruthven, we needed another plan and we needed it fast. We had to work and make some money if we were to have any hope of making a go of it on our own. We wanted a home and a family, so we took stock and eventually we decided to return to what we already knew. We decided we would be farmers.

FIFTY ACRES OF NEAR POVERTY

*Farming looks mighty easy when your plow is a pencil
and you're a thousand miles from the cornfield.*
—Dwight D. Eisenhower

With our general-store-managing days now well behind us, Frances and I purchased a small 50-acre farm just south of Blyth. Fran was never a big fan of this first farm (or farming in general), but for a young couple starting out, it was the best we could do. Our first years together were wonderful and difficult. We enjoyed each other's company, worked hard and as one example of the many challenges we faced together, Fran had a bout of rubella, a virus that is also known as German measles. While rubella is not generally life threatening in adults, when any sickness hits 50 percent of a farm's workforce, the practical impact is serious.

Gone were the days of horses. This was the modern era of farming.
Here I am on an 8N Ford Tractor.

In those first years farming, we raised weaner pigs (pigs that are sold at approximately 6 weeks after being weaned from their mother), cropped the land, and as a supplemental source of income, I drove truck for Howson and Howson delivering feed to area farms. We stayed on this farm near Blyth for about three years before selling it. We both wanted and needed to upsize, so when a 150-acre farm went on the auction block across from my father's place, we jumped at the opportunity to buy. This new farm, north of Auburn, was larger and had a lot more earning potential but also required much more work to make it all happen.

Despite these new demands on our personal time, this was the point at which we decided to start our family. On September 20, 1953, our daughter, Patricia Anne, was born. Patricia was followed on September 17, 1955, by her brother, Robert Wayne. Obviously children introduce an entirely new set of joys and challenges into any home, and Wayne and Patricia were no exception.

Frances, Wayne and Patricia. My new family in 1957.

Over and above the addition of children into our already busy lives, as had been our custom during past career ventures we never failed to diversify our income sources. This is actually a fancy way of saying we were always trying to make an extra nickel in whatever way we could.

Given that the Auburn farm had a small maple bush on the west side of the property near the Maitland River, it only seemed logical to jump into the maple syrup business.

My father liked making syrup, so he set about purchasing and procuring an evaporator and the other necessary elements of sap harvesting and syrup production. It wasn't long before our makeshift, handcrafted sugar shanty was the centre of a growing syrup empire. Each spring we tapped approximately 100 trees, which collectively yielded a few gallons of quality syrup, just enough to keep our family and friends flipping pancakes for the year. At the time we sold the syrup for about $4 per gallon—a profit that would be as much as 10 times higher if we were still producing and selling it today.

Inasmuch as the little bit of extra money was nice, more than the syrup profits I actually looked forward to the spring sap run for other reasons. Our modest sugar shanty was something that seemed to grow into a social endeavour. On the weekends, when we had the evaporator running, friends, family members and neighbours would gather in the bush to help with the collection of sap, the filling of the evaporator tank and the stoking of the fire, but while we accomplished the work, music was inevitably and inextricably part of the syrup process.

Father tends to the evaporator while Grandma and others look on.

While our small, economically challenged syrup business was primitive when compared to the larger, more efficient, reverse-osmosis, pipeline operations in place today, it offered something today's setups cannot give. It was something hands-on to do in the spring before seeding began, it gave us a chance to shake off the winter doldrums and it offered us a sweet opportunity to enjoy some music and frivolity with friends and family.

Our sugar shack was a meeting place for all—a home away from home.

As enjoyable as the Auburn farm was, just six short years after we said our wedding vows, Frances and I decided that living at or below the poverty line was not something we could continue to do. Our growing family needed more and so did we. We quickly sold the farm to Father, who many years later sold it to my brother Norman. Norman and his wife still live on that farm today, but for me, 1956 was the end of my farming days.

The week following the sale of the farm, I landed a job with Radford Construction in Blyth, but there was still the matter of our residence. Just before we sold the farm, Fran's father, Frank Hollyman, died suddenly of a massive heart attack. The unexpected loss of her father hit Frances hard, and as a result Frances wanted to move back in with her mother to help with the running of the house. Fran's mother, Mary, was an immaculate housekeeper, so we were somewhat worried over how she might adjust to the addition of four extra housemates, particularly when two of those housemates were energetic toddlers. We talked about the arrangement, and on paper it sounded like a good idea. Despite the pre-move assurances, with two very young children constantly running about in a very small house, the day-to-day family relationship with Mary quickly deteriorated. I suppose she was used to peace and quiet, but as anyone with children will understand, peace and quiet is often in short supply.

1961: Wayne and Patricia continued to grow.
We needed a space of our own.

In order to prevent real problems from emerging, I started looking for a new place to call home. In short order, the McIlroy house, which was located immediately beside Radford's, appeared on the market. I moved quickly and we purchased the quaint, three-bedroom, siding- and stucco-covered "foursquare" home.

The McClinchey family home on Queen Street in Blyth.

A short time after that, Frances was hired to work at the Blyth Canadian Imperial Bank of Commerce. With the income from Fran's job at the bank mixed with my reliable albeit meagre 90 cents per hour income from Radford's (a job I held for 10 years from 1956 to 1966), things were finally starting to look up for us.

Building a Future

*One of the things I learned the hard way was that it doesn't
pay to get discouraged. Keeping busy and making optimism
a way of life can restore your faith in yourself.*
—Lucille Ball

Between 1956 and 1966, I worked for the locally based Radford's
Construction. This was probably the place that I stayed the longest
save for the years that I worked for myself. I started my career at
Radford's hauling gravel in the southwestern Ontario townships of
Morris, Hullett and Elderslie, to name only a few of my destinations,
for a wage of 90 cents per hour. Most of the work was local, which
allowed me to be home every night, but whenever we worked in
Elderslie Township we stayed all week at the cookhouse because it
was too far to commute daily. As much as this was no big deal in my
youth, as a man with a family I now preferred being home with more
regularity. Fortunately, during the winter months I was posted much
closer to home. As a snowplow operator, I typically plowed snow in East
Wawanosh Township, but whenever I wasn't on the road, I worked in
the shop overhauling and maintaining the trucks and machines getting
ready for the next big blast of winter.

Back in the days when we had snow.

Everything needed to be kept in top working order. In the early years we still used trucks to push snow off the roads but eventually Radford's purchased graders for the job. I suspect they went to graders in an effort to save on labour. With trucks you needed both a driver and a wingman, but with graders one operator could do it all. Despite the potential savings, I didn't notice a bump in my paycheque.

In those days, especially during the winters of the late 1950s, the snowfall was particularly heavy, so it seemed like the plows and graders were constantly running.

It seemed as though the plows ran nonstop in those days.

There were a lot of roads to keep open and it was a difficult if not impossible job to keep everyone happy. I remember one of our biggest complainers. His name was Ernie Parker and he lived in a house on the Third Line of East Wawanosh Township. Ernie was convinced that we filled his lane with snow on purpose, and every time there was a storm, we knew there would be trouble. Ernie parked his car on the side of the road, which made our snow clearing job more difficult but allowed Ernie much easier access to the road. Ironically, as soon as the road was cleared enough for Ernie to drive to town, he would make the trip to report to our boss what a terrible job we had done clearing the snow in front of his house. I was never sure whether I should laugh at him or choke him into submission. This ritual became something we could rely on with one notable exception. One dark and snowy night, when visibility was next to zero, we were tasked with clearing the Third Line. By pure happenstance the wing caught the side of Ernie's car and flipped it over into the ditch. He was incensed and claimed we did it intentionally. Of course we didn't intend for it to happen but the accident did delay Ernie from making his traditional pilgrimage to complain.

After a couple of years hauling gravel and plowing snow, I was assigned the task of running a dipper-stick shovel feeding the crusher. I operated a Northwest for two years and then, following that, was put on a new Link Belt. Little did I know that these new duties would eventually send me back to the classroom for the first time since my teens.

Apparently the Department of Labour required anyone operating these machines to hold a valid hoisting licence. George Radford suggested I should get my paperwork in order, so I headed off to class.

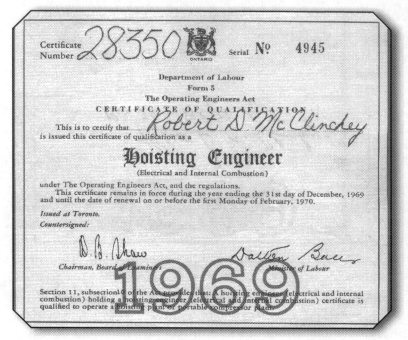

My hoisting license was my ticket to a new job.

After a brief study period in Toronto, I successfully completed the required exam in 1961. This certification allowed me to operate shovels, cranes and similar machines. As an augmentation to this ability, in April 1964 I also enrolled in the Chicago vocational training course in Toronto for a diesel and auto mechanic's ticket. With 92 percent on my entry exam, I was quickly accepted and eventually completed the program with a combined general average of 85 percent. I may still have had a lot to learn but it seems as though I had a good starting basis when it came to mechanics.

My diploma.

With this additional training and certification under my belt, I was eager to expand my duties once again. When I returned to Blyth, I resumed working at Radford's, where I operated everything from bulldozers and drag lines to front-end loaders and gravel trucks. Finally, George Radford put me on a Gradall excavator.

Running a dipper stick shovel was one of my many duties at Radford's.

For two years I worked on this infernal machine, and in that time I came to appreciate that of all the machines I had worked on, this was the one I liked the least. After two summers stuck on the Gradall, in 1966 I asked George for something else—anything else. Unfortunately he didn't have any openings at the time so I once again started looking for another line of work. As a point of interest, while I started my time at Radford's 10 years earlier, being paid 90 cents per hour, I concluded my tenure there earning only $1.10. In that time I had upgraded my skills, worked hard and missed very little time. Despite this, each time I asked for even a small raise in pay, George would respond with the same diatribe. "If I pay you more I have to raise everyone's wages and I can't afford that as I'm losing money every day." I guess everyone builds his empire his own way.

A Super Test

By working faithfully eight hours a day you may eventually
get to be boss and work twelve hours a day.
—Robert Frost

At this point in my life I had worked nearly 40 years for someone else. Through my labours I had helped to enrich others while, at the same time, my family and I continued to struggle to make ends meet. Sure, times were not as difficult as they had once been, but I longed for something more. I wanted a bigger piece of the pie and I wanted to be my own boss.

After I returned to Blyth from a futile job-hunting trip at my brother Bill's in British Columbia, I caught wind of a possible opportunity to own my own business right in the heart of Blyth. I heard that the Supertest garage in Blyth was listed for sale, and with my specific talents it seemed like a good fit. I approached Ben Walsh, the owner and operator of the business, and in the spring of 1967 I became the proud owner of a Supertest garage and gas station. At nearly the same time, the old one-room schools started the process of amalgamation into the larger style schools we know today. This systemic change required bussing, and as the routes came up for tender, I decided to leap into that business too. Without thinking much further, I submitted a bid on six of the new routes and was subsequently awarded three of them. My success in the tendering process now required me to purchase three new 60-passenger Bluebird schoolbuses. It also meant that I had to hire licensed drivers and certified mechanics to bring it all together. In a very short time I'd waded far into the world of independent business management and ownership. With any luck, this time we would fare better than we had in Ruthven.

Three new buses ready for the road.

At that time Blyth was a bustling business hub. In the late 1960s there were more than 40 different merchants within the community, and now I was one of them.

My son, Wayne, was only 12 years old at the time but he wanted to help with the budding family business. He was still going to elementary school but eagerly started helping around the garage by washing buses and sweeping up. Little did I know that Wayne would eventually make his career as a mechanic and many years after that would purchase the family business, which would come to be known as *McClinchey South End Auto*.

My garage years were good years. As always we worked hard but always found time to laugh and enjoy the fruits of our labours. I remember a man by the name of Norm Gowing. Norm owned a Sunoco gas station across the road. Despite being competitors of sorts, we had a pretty good relationship. We would even alternate the Sundays we stayed open. I would be open one weekend and he would be open the next. At least by working together we were able to get a day off every now and again.

The Blyth Business Association, 1969. (Front Row – Left to Right)
Doug Whitmore; Bill Hicks; Bill Thuell; Harold Vodden; Moody
Holland; Del Philip; Moe Wineberg; John Bailey; Norm Gowing; Bill
Knox; Archie Montgomery; (Middle) Alvin Snell; Bob McClinchey; Bill
King; Grant Sparling; Harvey Snell; Lloyd Walsh; John Manning; Bill
Howson; John Elliott; George Hubbard; Frank Bainton; George Hamm;
Jim Seid; Harve McCallum; John Campbell; Peter Reinsma; (Back)
George Radford; Harold Campbell; Stanley Chellew; Tom Cronin; Jack
Stewart; Jim Howson; Fred Howson; Lloyd Tasker; Ray Madill; George
Hamm Jr.; Borden Cook; Dr. Richard Street and Gordon Elliott.

The garage business is an interesting one. It is based largely on
brand and customer loyalty, but it is also one that yields its share of fair-
weather customers. Some, like Charlie Stewart, would pick and choose
when and with whom he would do business, depending on his mood
at the time. Charlie lived in Blyth and drove a 1948 Dodge Coupe.
He used to come to my garage to have his battery, tires, oil changes
and most other repairs taken care of. Then, as soon as the repair was
finished, he would drive past my pumps across the street to the Sunoco
for a fill-up. This was more an irritant than it was a problem for me but I
do recall one day when I had the chance to let him know that I noticed
what he was doing. Charlie landed in my shop one day with a leaky
gas tank on his car. He asked me to take a look at it, which I did, and
then I promptly reported, "The damn Sunoco gas seems to be rotting

out your tank." He stood there for a bit, smiled and then continued as if I had never mentioned it.

We operated that garage as a Supertest station for seven years, and then, partway through our contract, Supertest was sold to British Petroleum. We sold our original gas bar/garage operation to Gwylum Griffiths in 1974. For now we were out of the garage business, but this was not to be the last McClinchey garage business in Blyth.

THE GRAND VIEW FROM HERE

*As a restaurateur, my job is to basically control the chaos and the
drama. There's always going to be chaos in the restaurant business.*
—Rocco DiSpirito

In 1974 I was out of the gas bar/garage business but I still operated
three school bus routes in the area. I was still looking for something to
fill the rather large economic void left by the end of Supertest when,
tragically, local restaurateur Edith Creighton passed away. Edith owned
the Grandview Lunch, a small restaurant at the crossroads of Queen's
Highway #4 and Huron County Road #25, and as a result of her death,
the establishment was placed on the market for sale. For nearly as long
as we had been together, I had heard Frances speak of a desire to own
a restaurant. Her parents had owned one in the past, and with this
convincing and nostalgic argument, Fran talked me in to buying the
Grandview. Our next business venture was already underway.

The Grandview Lunch in its heyday.

Two years after I bought the restaurant, given that there was more land than was actually needed for the restaurant itself, I severed off a parcel of the property and built a garage and bus barn on the south half of the lot. This arrangement allowed me to put all our business interests in the same general location and provided me with a place to better service the three buses we operated at the time. For obvious financial reasons we lived in the back of the restaurant in a small but detached apartment. A few years after we first opened the restaurant's doors, we purchased and parked a small house trailer on the north end of the garage lot in which we happily lived for many years.

While I helped out where I could, the whole of the restaurant operation was primarily Fran's domain. She cooked, ordered supplies, managed the staff and did just about everything else associated with the day-to-day operations. We were open seven days a week and the holidays were our busiest times, so vacation time became harder and harder to come by. We also operated a Shell gas bar attached to the restaurant, and with all we had going on, our trips to the family cottage started becoming fewer and farther between.

Prior to purchasing the restaurant, in about 1968 I purchased a cottage on Lake Huron, north of Goderich at Port Albert. My plan was to spend some weekend leisure time with the family on the lake. I had always enjoyed fishing, and now that I was in my forties, I was looking forward to returning to the hobby that had offered me so much enjoyment in my youth. We looked for a while and eventually found a cottage that was in our price range. It was small and needed some work but we scooped it up right away. The cottage was a great place to entertain and to kick back.

Our cottage in Port Albert.

After 1976, the year our first grandson was born, it was also a place for our extended and again growing family to enjoy with us. We spent countless weekends there, but as time marched on, I found that the grass cutting, repairs and general maintenance seemed to take precedence over the fishing and fun. Our lives were getting busier, more hectic, and after we bought the restaurant, the cottage was far less convenient and leisurely that it had originally been. In 1984, 16 years after we had first set out the welcome mat, we sold the cottage and moved on.

Grandmother Anderson and I share a
moment in the canoe by the cottage.

Our cottage was a great place to entertain. Here we are—Father,
Bob Dayman, Mother, Thelma Dayman and me in August 1977.

The Grandview Lunch was largely a successful business, but it was one that was demanding and unrelenting from time and energy perspectives. Frances and I were getting older and the prospect of increasing our workload was not something we relished. As a result, in December 1981 we sold the business to Ross and Erma Brighton. We moved permanently to the house trailer and focused our efforts and attention on the three bus routes we'd held since 1967.

BACK TO BUS-NESS

*The person whose problems are all behind them
is probably a school bus driver.*
—Author Unknown

In 1976 I took steps to sever a parcel of land off our restaurant property. My intention at the time was to construct a garage and a bus barn on the south half of the lot. This arrangement would permit me to geographically consolidate our business interests but also provide me with a place to better service the three buses that we operated at the time. The only problem with my plan was that the lot I severed was low and swampy and needed a great deal of preparatory work. As a result, before we could start construction, we need to find, haul and place a great deal of fill. I had the skills but not the equipment, so I went on a bit of a shopping spree. I bought a used Massey front-end loader and a backhoe from Stewart Johnston. I also found a small gravel truck that, after a few repairs at the garage in Mitchell, was just what we needed to start working on the bus barn.

Once I had all the equipment I started hauling fill and eventually had enough to adequately raise and level the ground under the site of the soon-to-be bus barn. As a fortunate happenstance, a few years later the village of Blyth installed municipal sewage systems, so there was an abundance of fill that needed to be dumped somewhere. My property was a convenient location, so in very short order I had enough fill to level the entire property.

The bus barn was 88 feet long and 40 feet wide and contained a 28-foot-long pit and a hydraulic hoist to raise and lower small passenger vehicles. I hired my son, Wayne, in 1979 as a bus driver, and given that he was a licensed mechanic, he was also able to help with a few repairs as needed. This arrangement worked well and allowed Frances and me to occasionally get away for holidays. This notion of time off was a big change from our years in the restaurant business.

Generally speaking, the bus business was good for us. We had numerous drivers during our 25 years in business, but the most dedicated was certainly my sister-in-law Lila. With the exception of one or two years in the beginning, Lila was behind the wheel at McClinchey Bus Lines for the entire quarter century, and she kept things running smoothly. Her bus was always clean and she was a good and dependable driver who set the tone during the run. Put another way, the kids on Lila's bus knew it was best to stay on her sunny side. In many ways, this was a lesson the rest of us understood too.

One of my other drivers was my wife, Frances. She was dependable but didn't always enjoy winter driving. One year while she was traversing the slippery and snow-covered Huron County roads, she misjudged a stop and collided with the back end of a minister's car. Fortunately no one was injured, the bus was completely undamaged and the car required only minor repairs, which is more than I can say for Fran's reputation in the years following the incident. From that moment on, whenever you wanted to rile Frances up, you only had to whisper the phrase "Crash McClinchey."

My sister Eileen and my son, Wayne, also drove for McClinchey Bus Lines, and I am tremendously thankful for their work over the years. We never had a serious accident and not one child was hurt on our watch, a record I am proud of and thankful for. With the exception of the big snowstorm of 1971, we picked up and delivered our kids each day safely and without serious incident. I say with the exception of the storm in 1971 because that winter the students were stranded at school for the better part of a week. After the teachers were trapped in the schools with the "little darlings" for 120 hours straight, I found the buses were cancelled far more frequently in the winters following.

As an interesting aside, we also transported kids to swimming lessons in Vanastra (the former Canadian Forces Base, located outside the town of Clinton) during the summer months. I only mention this because it was on one of those trips between Blyth and Vanastra that our oldest grandson, Greg, met his future wife, Julie McNichol. While it was not evident during their first meeting, this chance encounter aboard my bus led to their marriage, which is now going on its 11th year.

In 1989, after more than a generation on the road, I sold the buses and the routes to Murphy Bus Lines in Clinton. McClinchey Bus Lines closed its doors forever.

WEDNESDAY NIGHT CLASS

*A studio recording is perfection, but emotion and passion come
only when you turn on the machine and go for the groove.
If you do that with no mistakes, it sounds beautiful.*

—Chuck Mangione

Somewhere around 1955, when I was in my late twenties, my uncle Tom Anderson gave me a nice Stainer Fiddle for Christmas. Uncle Tom was my mother's brother, and he gave me the Stainer because he knew of my deep interest in playing music but also understood that I wasn't typically allowed to play with Father's violin. Oddly enough, I was nearly thirty years of age, I had intensely loved music for my entire life and I was only now starting to learn to play.

Despite my late start on the fiddle, it turned out that music was to be one of the most important and constant components in my life. As a child at home, music was the pastime that brought our family together nearly every day after supper; as a teen, a dance in Blyth is where I first met my future wife; and as an adult, music allowed me to establish, build and maintain associations with some of my closest friends.

As I have already noted, when I was a young man, I played in concerts for numerous events, community festivals and at dances throughout the area. I can even remember playing with Father at a few square dances—something that seems to have died out in our more modern satellite radio world. To some that might seem inconsequential, but I view it as being really unfortunate because had it not been for community dances such as that, I may never have met Elgin Fisher.

On Saturday nights in the 1960s I regularly attended music evenings at the Commercial Hotel in Seaforth. On one particular January 19 (I remember the date because that night in question happened to be my birthday), a group of us headed off for a night on the town. Elgin Fisher was the featured entertainer that night so it was sure to be good. During one of Elgin's many breaks, he happened to stumble over to our table. He sat down, introduced himself and declared that this very night was his birthday. Of course it was my birthday too so, after a bit of good natured ribbing over which of us appeared to be older (Elgin was clearly the one who looked older as I maintained a very youthful appearance), we discovered that we were exactly the same age. At that point a conversation erupted and a friendship developed. I am pleased to say that our friendship has endured many years and even still, Elgin and I play music and visit quite regularly. I am also pleased to say that he still appears much older than I do.

I think we can all agree that Elgin (left) and Bob (right) both look older than I do.

In the years that followed, my relationship with Elgin was one that grew largely because of our common interest in performing. Not long after we met, we brought a small group of musicians together. Elgin, Bruce Ryan and I used to practise at each other's homes generally once a month. Once we revved up our talents, we started performing at local nursing homes. Some have suggested that we started playing at nursing homes because many of the residents couldn't hear what we really sounded like, but more accurately I think they truly enjoyed our light and unique style all the same. Pinecrest Manor in Lucknow; Huronview in Clinton; Huronlea in Brussels; Queensway in Hensall; Goderich Place in Goderich and a host of others regularly opened their doors for our group, the Nashville Rejects, to play for their residents.

Wayne McClinchey, Bob McClinchey and Elgin Fisher entertain the patrons at the Royal Canadian Legion in Goderich.

Elgin and Bruce played and sang while I backed them up on the fiddle. For the most part we had a semi-regular repertoire that we used while playing the so-called circuit, but I remember once while we were on stage when Elgin veered off course.

The Nashville Rejects take the stage for a crowd of local seniors in 1995.

Elgin, who we often called "the Boss," enjoyed the Ray Charles hit "Born to Lose." Despite the less than inspirational words associated with the tune, Elgin suggested that a nursing home would be a good place to perform the song, a song that goes something like this:

All I see is only loneliness
All my life I've always been so blue
Born to lose and now I'm losing you
Born to lose and now I'm losing you

As you can see, the song is certainly not inspirational, particularly for a group of long-term-care residents who may not enjoy the message of impending death contained within the song. Eventually I managed to convince Elgin that this one might be more appropriate in another location.

Notwithstanding the occasional bump, the Nashville Rejects were largely successful. Then, one day it occurred to us that our group might be missing something. We needed a bass player so we managed to get Bob Mann on the ticket. Fortunately, given his particular skill set and abilities, Bob was "between jobs" (as he liked to put it), and while with

Bob Mann as part of our group some might argue that we are still missing something, he has been a great friend to us over the years.

Bob Mann tries to keep up with Elgin and me.

It was also during this time period that Elgin talked me into joining the Goderich No Notes. This off-colour jug band consisted of about a dozen guys, each clad in overalls and odd hats, singing and playing instruments such as the gut-bucket, harmonicas, the spoons, guitars and fiddles. I enjoyed the lighthearted, hillbilly motif, but more than that I liked that we travelled throughout the area playing in parades, at concerts and at a host of other events and venues.

The Goderich No Notes were not known for their fashion sense.

It was a great few years, but after a while a few of the key players moved on, passed on or otherwise lost interest. The Goderich No Notes eventually disbanded but the friendships lasted a lifetime.

Sadly, in 1998, one of the founding members of the Nashville Rejects, Bruce Ryan, passed away. While we miss him, the rest of our group's members have continued playing with each other up to this very day. While as of 2003 we no longer play the nursing home circuit, the large and spacious lounge in my son's shop serves as a frequent backdrop for our music nights. We also alternate between the respective homes of the various members of our group. We now play once a month, and unless someone new happens to join us for the night as a guest, we typically have about eight players at our monthly sessions: four or five guitar players, two fiddlers and a steel-guitar player. For a lark, in 2004, the group, which was comprised of Ken Scott, Bob Mann, Bill MacDougall, Wayne McClinchey, Elgin Fisher and me, released a pseudo-recording that was compiled and mixed by another friend and frequent participant in our music nights, Harry Busby. This time we nicknamed our group "Wednesday Night Class."

Wednesday Night Class in 2011. Steve Argyle,
Bob Mann, Bob McClinchey,
Wayne McClinchey, Elgin Fisher, Bill MacDougall and Harry Busby.

Wednesday Night Class is a social cluster, a musical grouping, and if you ask Bob Mann, it is a poetry circle. Bob routinely prepares and presents his own uniquely inspired creative work. Given the context, I have included one such piece below:

Elgin Our Boss
Sang and played a Martin guitar; and drove us around in his lovely white car.
Sometimes it would get dirty when we met a big truck.
Elgin would get annoyed, but Bob and I didn't give a ... damn.
Yes, Elgin was the captain of a ship that was robust.
He collected all our pay and must still hold it all in trust.

Another couple Frances and I frequently associated with was Jack and Elva Armstrong. We went on several camping trips with Jack and Elva, who owned a nice 23-foot boat.

Fran and I take a ride with Jack and Elva on the boat.

As a matter of course, we usually went up the Bruce Peninsula to the Wiarton or Tobermory areas to camp, fish or sightsee on Georgian Bay. In the fall of 1984 we sold our Dodge motor home, and the next spring we purchased a 28-foot motor home, on a Ford chassis, as a replacement.

The Armstrong boat and the McClinchey motor home.
Great summers on wheels.

That spring we were invited to camp at Joe Freeman's place, which was called the Shepparton Shuffle. During our stay, through playing music, we were introduced to an entirely new group of musicians. This group held several campouts each year and they invited us to start attending regularly. There were campers from London, Shakespeare, Brantford, Goderich and all points in between. Most were very musical and/or were accomplished entertainers in their own right. As part of this circle, we attended numerous fiddle and music jamborees in Shelburn, Stratford, Tavistock, Dorchester and many more places.

Our circle of musical friends continued to grow.

Once we became established within this new group, we also invited them to Blyth to participate in and partake of the annual Huron Pioneer Thresher and Hobby Association Show, a big part of which was musical performances. They would usually show up on the Friday, spend Friday and Saturday night, have a few tunes and drinks on our lawn and then head home. It didn't get much better than that. That was until the summer of 1998.

That year my son, Wayne, set up some recording equipment in his garage. Then, with much prodding and Wayne's accompaniment on the guitar, I grabbed my fiddle and started to play. Over the course of the following several weeks, Wayne and I would play six or eight songs per night. We often made mistakes and had to redo the number but eventually we had cleanly recorded 50 songs. At that point, the project seemed to drop from the radar. That was until the following Christmas when Wayne surprised me with something really special.

Recording in the garage—an experience to remember.

Unknown to me Wayne had taken the time to add bass, drums, the mandolin and a banjo to our recordings. After he sufficiently dressed up the songs, he packaged them and prepared a two-volume set of tapes with 25 songs on each tape. He called it "Me and My Fiddle." When I first listened to the recordings I was really shocked. He had obviously put in countless hours of painstaking work because I actually sounded good. Even more flattering was the fact that he had given me a number of extra copies to sell or give to my friends and soon-to-be fans. So with the combined efforts of Wayne, Harry Busby (digital engineering), Kelly Cook (cover design) and Greg and Julie McClinchey (subsequent recording and graphic services), my debut as a budding recording artist was official. The tapes and eventually CDs sold quite well in the area, but my success in the recording industry was not so great as to allow the money to corrupt me (unfortunately).

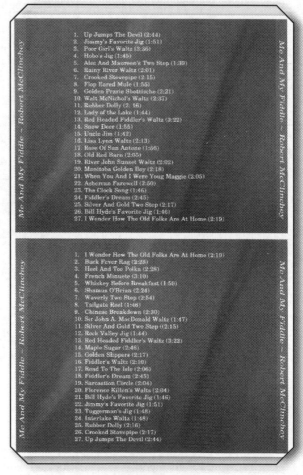

The list of songs on my CDs.

The CD cover picture.

But again, none of these experiences would have taken place had my uncle Tom Anderson not first given me that Stainer Fiddle as a Christmas gift back in 1955. Looking back over the past 86 years, I know I owe him a great deal.

Uncle Tom Anderson.

One Last Home Together

A kiss makes the heart young again and wipes out the years.
—Rupert Brooke

After selling McClinchey Bus Lines in 1989, Frances and I finally decided to retire. We sold our property and our remaining business interests to our son, Wayne, and his then common-law partner, Jackie Lantinga. McClinchey South End Auto was born and suddenly my little bus barn was a second-generation family business. Fran and I used the proceeds from that sale to purchase a nice cottage-style house and large in-town property at 226 McConnell Street East, in Blyth. The house, which was located on the north side of McConnell Street, was solid and clean; it had a single car garage and a car port and lots of room for Fran and me to spread out.

226 McConnell Street in Blyth. Our new home.

The large double lot meant there was always yard work to do, but I enjoyed having something to putter at. Between cutting the grass, pruning the hedges and keeping the house up to snuff, I was always busy. We were still close to Wayne's—close enough for me to help out when I wanted but far enough away that I could stay hidden when I didn't.

In addition to the location, I also enjoyed that we still had the space to accommodate our friends and their mobile homes and campers. In particular, when the Thresher's weekend rolled around each September, our place was a popular camping locale. We were just a few blocks from the main fairgrounds so we wouldn't miss a second of the action at the annual show. Some years we played host to a dozen or more campers, each bringing their instruments with them. For at least that one weekend each September, the Opry Stage had nothing on our little corner of the earth.

After we formally retired we finally had the time we needed to visit with our friends whenever we wanted. I should also mention that our family again expanded with the addition of a toy poodle named Beau. Beau was immediately Fran's pride and joy—next to me that is. The three of us travelled to fiddle jamborees, plowing matches and camping weekends all over the area. It was a great time for us, and with the acquisition of our own motor home, nothing could stop us.

Fran also used the time to do some of her favourite things. She enjoyed playing bingo, general shopping and going on the mail route with our daughter, Patricia. I didn't mind that she was away a lot so long as she was still able to drive herself. I enjoyed my freedom and would not have preferred to be the chauffer to Friday afternoon bingo games. I also think that Fran enjoyed her own independence and freedom. We seemed to have the best of both worlds, spending quality time together and pursuing our individual interests separately. But all this changed in late 1996.

In 1996 the Blyth Public School hosted a reunion for former students and staff. The attendance was quite good and the event was a huge success. Frances, a former student at the Blyth School, truly enjoyed seeing her former classmates and reminiscing about past friends, old memories and days gone by. After the reunion events wrapped up,

Frances came home and went to bed. That night, she awoke with dizzy spells and a very high temperature. We had arranged to go camping the next day but she was in such a terrible state that we needed to cancel the plans. Frances eventually saw a doctor, and he diagnosed her with an inner-ear problem, but I always suspected that it was something worse than that. I don't know if she picked up a virus or what the problem was but, from that day on, she was never the same.

While Frances was a smoker in her younger days, as she got older she took her habit underground. As a careful closet smoker she never smoked in front of me, so I figured she had shaken the habit. She may have butted out for a time, but given that all of her bingo cronies and shopping pals were heavy chain smokers, Frances eventually lit up again. Most of the family knew of her habit, but for some strange reason she didn't want me to know. Soon the intense and debilitating coughing started, and with her unstable balance getting worse, it wasn't long before she was fully homebound. As her list of medications grew longer, her stamina and ability to get around seemed to get shorter. Puffers, pills and even part-time oxygen started to drain the life from the young and vibrant woman I once met on the dance floor at a party at the Blyth Hall all those years ago. Eventually, following a close call as a result of a Boxing Day bout of heart failure, Frances required oxygen on a full-time basis, something that lasted for her final two or three years. Needless to say I stuck pretty close to home for those final years, and our travelling and camping trips stopped cold. I missed those times, but as a result of her illness, I became the chief cook and bottle washer around the house in those days. Fran couldn't do too much, so most of the work and daily chores fell to me.

By this time, Wayne had remarried a great lady named Dorothy (née Nicholson). Dorothy was a tremendous help during this period and I am not sure I could have done it without her.

Fran and I pose with our son, Wayne, and his new wife,
Dorothy, on their wedding day. They were married at their
Hullett Township home on Christmas Eve, 2005.

Despite my efforts to give her the best of care, Frances ended up in
the Clinton Hospital with lung cancer. On April 8, 2008, she passed
quietly into the light.

My Miss Frances and our dog Beau. Fran was
still the prettiest girl I have ever seen.

On April 9, 2008, for the first time in more than 60 years, Frances and I were separated. We had been married for 58 years and it was quite a shock to see it all end. I will never forget our time together and will always be grateful for those years we had. Even after all the time had passed, she was still the most beautiful girl I had ever set eyes on.

After Fran was gone I decided I would stay in our house for at least one more year. My independence was important and I wanted to see if I still had both the health and desire to maintain a house of my own.

After a year passed, I made a decision. Cooking for one was no fun and I simply had too much space for just myself. After Fran had died, Wayne and Dorothy offered me a wonderful three-bedroom apartment within their home. The deal was to include my meals and laundry, and most importantly of all, company when I wanted it and solitude and privacy when I needed it. I really wasn't keen on the idea at first, but after I considered all the factors involved, it seemed like a great offer. After a bit more conversation, I agreed to make the move. To get ready for the transition, on May 27, 2009, with the help of my family and musical friends, we held an auction sale at my house on McConnell. Prior to the sale, I gave a large portion of our things to family and friends, but as anyone who moves knows, you can accumulate a lot of stuff in just a few short years.

I moved into my new apartment on June 1, 2009, and much to the chagrin of my daughter, Patricia, I soon after sold the house to my grandson Greg and his wife, Julie (and their two children Mieka and Koby). Patricia disowned me at this point, refusing to acknowledge or speak to me because I didn't give her the house. This really bothered me at first, but time is a great healer. While it is too bad Patricia has opted to cut me out of her life, I don't intend to lose any more sleep over it. These are her decisions, and while I still love her, I will not permit her inward thinking to negatively impact my life.

I have been living in my new apartment for nearly four years and am happy and content. I go out to the shop nearly every day for coffee with Wayne and any shop visitors; I cut grass and do other light jobs when there is a need; and I maintain my independence and hobbies. I still play the fiddle regularly with a group of good friends; I watch the odd baseball game; and I pretty much come and go as I please.

My living room window faces south, which offers a good view in the direction of my first farm. Dorothy is a tremendous cook and makes sure that I have a hot meal in the evening. The family's German shepherds and Sylvester the cat visit with me regularly, and after 80 years of sacrifice and work, I have the freedom that I always worked for. This is living.

Epilogue

I did it my way.
—Frank Sinatra

After celebrating my 85th birthday, and through the coaxing of certain friends and members of my family, it occurred to me that maybe I should try to write my memoirs while I still have a few of my marbles left (assuming it is not already too late). I know my memory had diminished somewhat but I have tried, to the best of my ability, to recall several of the important, funny, pleasant and difficult times of my life. It has been an enjoyable experience to write this book, and I truly hope that readers enjoy it as much as I have enjoyed putting it together. It is a selective and condensed version of my nearly ninety years of living, but with any luck I will get to add a few more chapters in the years ahead.

Looking back, I have come to understand that I am fortunate to have been born in an era when a handshake was as good as a contract and neighbours could always be counted on to help when the chips were down. Granted, money was harder to come by in my youth, but at the same time, pennies could be stretched much further than they can today. There was a time when many of us struggled to keep our head above water, particularly in the "dirty thirties" when everyone seemed to be fighting just to make ends meet. Despite the scarcity of cash, for the most part we were happy. Many say those were terrible times, but I know that I was fortunate to have lived through them.

When I finished school I didn't have to worry about getting a job. On the contrary, when I finished school I was able to work at several different jobs because skilled labour was scarce. The war years were likewise challenging, but again, they provided me with several opportunities to meet new and interesting people, to acquire new skills and to partake of hands-on learning while I worked.

I understand that today, it is not uncommon for someone to train for a specific job and to then spend an entire life working at that one job. This might be a good system for some but it would not have been the way that I would have wanted it. I value the diversity of my life and working experiences and consider those experiences to be important and defining characteristics of who I was and have become.

Four generations of the McClinchey family—and still growing.

Perhaps paycheques and bank accounts are now bigger than mine were, but even with the allure of more money, I wouldn't have changed my life path for all the tea in China. Money is great and it certainly helps make the world go 'round, but, as the saying goes, you can't take it with you. Money can't be the driving force in your life if your goal is happiness and fulfilment. If money had been my main motivator, the pages of this book would be bland and frankly not worth the read.

As far as regrets, I have a few. I would have liked to have taken more music training earlier in my life, for example. If I could give any advice to young kids today, it would be to pick up an instrument. Music is the key to the soul, and for me, playing the fiddle was when I was most at peace with myself. Music has always been a great joy in my life. It brought me friends, kept my sanity and in a very real way introduced me to my wife of 58 years.

I am now in my 87th year, and looking back on my life so far, I have to smile. I have been a fisherman, a pool hustler, a machinist, a mechanic, an ice-road trucker, a gas station attendant, a builder of roads, a snowplow operator, a bus driver, a syrup maker, a farmer, a husband, a father, a grandfather and even a great-grandfather, and I am still trying to figure out what I want to be when I grow up. Perhaps my mother, in her gentle and infinite wisdom, summed me up best when she said, "Bob ... you are a jack of all trades and a master of none."

Cheers to the years ahead.

Appendix i

In 1830, Robert and Mary (née Rathwell) McClinchey, along with their four young children (Agnes, Henry, James and Matthew) left their home in County Down, Ireland, and set sail for a new life in Canada. The McClinchey family settled in southern Ontario and, since those very first days, have continued to make their homes predominantly in the Huron and Bruce County regions of the province. Today, the oldest direct living descendant of the aforementioned Robert McClinchey is Robert Donald McClinchey (born in 1926) and the youngest is Koby Aiden McClinchey (born in 2008), making them the fifth and eighth generations of Canadian McClincheys, respectively.

In 2011, the McClinchey family was recognized by the Governor General of Canada for 180 years of residency in Canada. The citation is attached below.

Canada was built through the hard work and dedication of its settlers who established communities and helped one another in common cause. It was with the hopes of a better life in mind that the McClinchey family settled in Ontario and set about contributing to their region and creating a lasting legacy to the country.

For 180 years, members of the McClinchey family have worked as doctors, farmers, mechanics, politicians, homemakers and soldiers, while ensuring that their traditions are passed on to subsequent generations. The people of the surrounding area have had their lives enriched by the presence of this family, as has Canada itself.

I would like to extend my warmest wishes to all those celebrating this remarkable milestone.

David Johnston

June 2011

Appendix 2

Robert Donald McClinchey   Born January 19, 1926
Frances Mary Hollyman   Born July 9, 1930
     Died April 8, 2008

Bob and Frances were married on May 27, 1950, and subsequently had two children.

Robert and Frances on their wedding day, May 27, 1950.

1. Patricia Anne McClinchey   Born September 20, 1953
2. Robert Wayne McClinchey   Born September 17, 1955

Wayne and Patricia in their early years, 1959.

Patricia married James Harold Brigham.

Patricia and Jim Brigham and their children, 1991.

Their union resulted in four children.

1. Jennifer Brigham   Born October 13, 1979
2. Mary Elizabeth Brigham   Born March 8, 1981
3. Kendra Brigham   Born August 11, 1983
4. Gordon Brigham   Born January 18, 1990

Jennifer, Kendra, Mary and Gordon Brigham, 1993.

Wayne married Glenda Darlene Bromley on July 20, 1974.

Wayne and Darlene say their vows, 1974.

The two divorced in 1981 but the union resulted in one child.

Gregory McClinchey   Born April 3, 1976

Wayne and Darlene with their new son, Greg, 1977.

Wayne married Dorothy Nicholson on December 24, 2005, in their Hullett Township home where they continue to reside.

Wayne and Dorothy exchange rings during their wedding, 2005.

Greg McClinchey married Julie McNichol on November 2, 2002.

Wayne, Greg and I take a moment and Julie McClinchey looks on, 2002.

This union resulted in two children.

1. Mieka McClinchey   Born November 29, 2005
2. Koby McClinchey   Born September 3, 2008

Greg and Julie and their children Mieka and Koby McClinchey, 2011.